GRIMOIRE
OF POPE
HONORIUS

Unicursal

Copyright © 2024

Translation by M-A Ricard

Éditions Unicursal Publishers
unicursal.ca

ISBN 978-2-89806-607-8 (Paperback)
ISBN 978-2-89806-608-5 (Hardcover)

First English Edition, Imbolc 2024

GRIMOIRE OF POPE HONORIUS

WITH A COLLECTION OF THE RAREST SECRETS

ROME

MDCLXX

GREMOIRE
DV PAPE HONORIVS.
AVEC VN RECVEIL
DES ELVS RARES.
SECRETS .

A ROME .

MDCLXX.

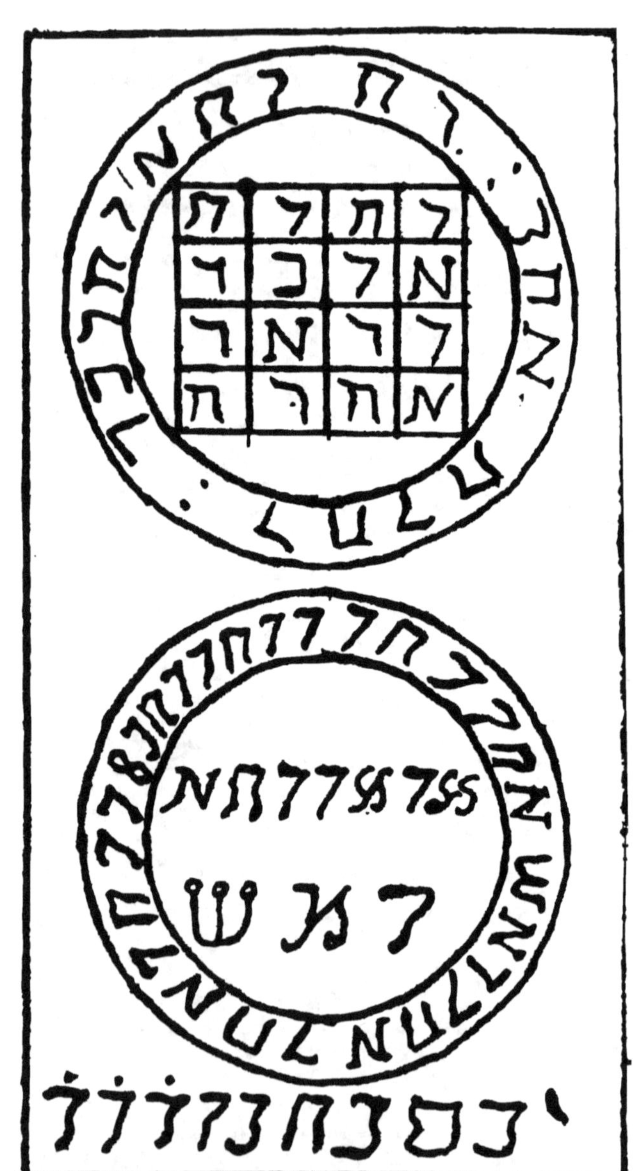

CONSTITUTIONS OF POPE HONORIUS THE GREAT,

In which are found the secret conjurations to be made against the Spirits of Darkness.

The Holy Apostolic See, to whom the keys of the Kingdom of Heaven have been given, by these words of Jesus Christ to Saint Peter: *I give you the keys of the Kingdom of Heaven*, to you alone the power to command the Prince of Darkness and his Angels, who as servants of their master, owe him honour, glory and obedience; by the other words of Jesus Christ: *The Lord only you shall serve;* by the power of the keys, the head of the Church has been made Lord of the underworld.

As until now, the Sovereign Pontiffs alone have had the power to call and command the Spirits. The Holiness of Honorius III, out of pastoral solicitude, has kindly accepted to communicate the manner and power of calling and commanding Spirits to his venerable brothers in Jesus Christ, adding the conjurations that must be made in such cases, all contained in the following bull:

HONORIUS,

Servant of the servants of God: To each and every one of our venerable brothers of the holy Roman Church, Cardinals, Archbishops, Bishops, Abbots; to each and every one of our sons in Christ, Priests, Deacons, Subdeacons, Acolytes, Exorcists, Readers, Porters, clerics, both secular and regular, greetings and Apostolic benediction. At the time when the Son of God, Saviour of the world, begotten before time, and born according to his humanity of the seed of David, lived on earth, whose most holy name is Jesus, before whom heaven, earth and hell must bow their knees, we saw with what power he commanded the Demons, which power was transmitted to Saint Peter, is Peter, and on this rock I will build my Church, and the gates of hell shall not prevail against it. These words were addressed to Saint Peter, as the head and foundation of the Church.

We, then, who by the mercy of God, in spite of our little merit, have attained the sovereign apostolate, and who, as the legitimate successor of Saint Peter, hold in our hands the keys to the Kingdom of Heaven, wishing to communicate the power to call and command the Spirits, which was reserved to us alone, and which our predecessors alone had enjoyed ; wishing, I say, to share it, by divine inspiration, with our venerable brothers and dear sons in Jesus Christ, lest in the exorcism of the possessed, they be terrified by the horrible figures of these rebellious angels, whom sin has thrown into the abyss and that they are not even sufficiently instructed in what to do and observe, and so those who have been redeemed by the blood of Jesus Christ, may not be afflicted by any evil, and possessed by the Devil, we have inserted, in this Bull, the manner of calling them, which must be inviolably observed; and because it is fitting that the Ministers of the Altars should have authority over rebellious Spirits, we grant them all the letters we have, in virtue of the Holy Apostolic See, on which we are mounted, and we order them, by our Apostolic authority, to inviolably observe the following, lest by a negligence unworthy of their character, they incur the wrath of the Almighty.

Whoever wishes to summon the Spirits of evil and of darkness, must spend three days fasting, confess and approach the Holy Altar. After these three days, he will recite the following day, at sunrise, the seven Gradual Psalms, with the Litanies and Orisons, all on his knees, and he must neither drink wine nor eat meat on that day. He will rise at midnight on the first

Monday of the month, and a priest will say a Mass of the Holy Spirit; after the consecration of the Host, taking it in his left hand, he shall recite the following Orison on his knees.

ORISON.

My Sovereign Jesus Christ, Son of the living God, Thou who for the salvation of all mankind didst suffer the death of the Cross; Thou who, before being abandoned to Thine enemies, by an impulse of ineffable love didst institute the Sacrament of thy Body; Thou who hast vouchsafed to us miserable creatures the privilege of making daily commemoration thereof; do Thou deign unto thine unworthy servant, thus holding thy Living Body in his hands, all strength and ability for the profitable application of that power with which he has been entrusted against the horde of rebellious Spirits. Thou art their true God, and if they tremble at the utterance of Thy Name, upon that Holy Name will I call, crying: Jesus Christ. Jesus, be Thou my help, now and for ever. Amen.

After sunrise a black Rooster must be killed, the first feather of its left wing being plucked and preserved for use at the required time. The eyes must be torn out, and so also the tongue and heart; these must be dried in the sun and afterwards reduced to powder. The remains must be interred at sunset in a secret place, a cross of a palm in height being set upon the mound, while at each of the four corners the signs which here follow must be drawn with the thumb:

On this day also the operator should drink no wine and abstain from eating meat.

On Tuesday, at break of day, let him say a Mass of the Angels, placing the feather taken from the Rooster upon the Altar, together with a new penknife. The signs hereinafter represented must be inscribed on a sheet of clean white paper with the consecrated wine which is the Blood of Jesus Christ:

√ I Z T W

They should be written upon the Altar, and at the end of the Mass the paper should be folded in a new veil of violet silk, to be concealed on the morrow, together with the Oblation of the Mass and a part of the consecrated Host.

On the evening of Thursday the operator must rise at midnight, and, having sprinkled holy water about the chamber, he must light a taper of yellow wax, which shall have been prepared on the Wednesday, which will be pierced in the form of a cross. And when it is lighted, he shall recite Psalm LXXVII: *Attendite, popule meus, legem meam*; et sans dire, *Gloria Patri*.

He shall then begin the Office of the Dead with: *Venite, exultemus Domino, &c.*

He shall recite Matins and Lauds; but in place of the versicle of the ninth Lesson, he shall say: *Libera me, Domine, de timore inferni; nequeant dæmones perdere animam meam, quando illos ab inferis suscitabo, dum illos velle meum imperabo.*

Which means: Deliver us, O Lord, from the fear of hell. Let not the Demons destroy my soul when I shall raise them from the deep pit, when I shall command them to do my will.

Dies illa sit clara, sol luceat et luna, quando illos suscitabo.

That is to say: May the day be bright and may the sun and moon shine forth, when I shall call upon them.

Tremendus illorum aspectus horribilis et difformis. Redde formam angelicam, dum illis velle meum imperabo.

That is to say: Terrible of aspect are they, deformed and horrible to sight; but do Thou restore unto them their angelic shapes when I shall impose my will upon them.

Libera me, Domine, de illis cum visu terribili, et præsta ut sint illi obedientes, quando illos ab inferis suscitabo, dum illis velle meum imperabo.

Lord deliver me from those of the dread visage, and grant that they shall be obedient when I shall raise them up from hell, when I shall impose my will upon them.

After the Office of the Dead, the operator shall extinguish the taper, and at sunrise shall cut the throat of a male Lamb of nine days, taking care that the blood does not gush forth upon the earth. He shall skin the Lamb, and shall cast its tongue and heart into the fire. The fire must be freshly kindled, and the ashes shall be preserved for use at the proper time. The skin of the Lamb shall be spread in the middle of a field, and for the space of nine days shall be sprinkled four times every day with holy water.

On the tenth day, before the rising of the sun, the lambskin shall be covered with the ashes of the heart and tongue, and with the ashes also of the Rooster.

On Thursday, after sunset, the flesh of the Lamb shall be interred in a secret place where no Bird can come, and the priest with his right thumb shall inscribe on the grave the characters here indicated:

Moreover, for the space of three days, he shall sprinkle the four corners with holy water, saying: *Asperges me, Domine, hissopo et mundabor, lavabis me et super nivem dealbabor.*

[That is to say: Sprinkle me, O Lord, with hyssop, and I shall be cleansed. Wash me, and I shall be made whiter than snow.]

After the aspersion, let him recite the following Orison, kneeling with his face towards the East.

Orison.

Jesus Christ, Redeemer of men, who, being the Lamb without stain, wast immolated for the salvation of the human race, who alone wast found worthy to open the Book of Life, impart such virtue to this lambskin that it may receive the signs which we shall trace thereon, written with Thy blood, so that the figures, signs, and words may become efficacious; and grant that this skin may preserve us against the wiles of the Demons; that they may be terrified at the sight of these figures, and may only approach them trembling. Through Thee, Jesus Christ, who livest and reignest through all ages. So be it.

The Litanies of the Holy Name of Jesus must then be repeated, but instead of the *Agnus Dei,* substitute:

Immolated Lamb, be Thou a pillar of strength against the Demons.

Slain Lamb, give power over the Powers of Darkness.

Immolated Lamb, grant favour and strength unto the binding of the Rebellious Spirits. So be it.

After the lambskin has been stretched for eighteen days, on the nineteenth day the fleece shall be removed, reduced into powder, and interred in the same place. The word *vellus* shall be written above it with the finger, together with the following character, and the words: *istud sic in cinerem reductum, si presidium contra dæmones per nomen Jesu.*

[That is to say: May this which hath been reduced into ashes preserve against the Demons through the name of Jesus.]
Then, also, these characters:

Lastly, on the Eastern side, the said skin must be set to dry in the sun for three days, the ensuing characters being cut with a new knife:

This being accomplished, recite Psalm LXXI: *Deus judicium tuum, regida, &c.,* and cut the following characters:

The figure being thus far completed, recite the verses *Offerte Domino patria gentium, &c.,* occurring in Psalm xcv., *Cantate Domino canticum,* of which the seventh versicle is: *offerte Domino filii Dei, &c.,* and cut subsequently these characters:

Next recite Psalm LXXVII: *Attendite popule meus, legem meam, &c.* and compose the following figure:

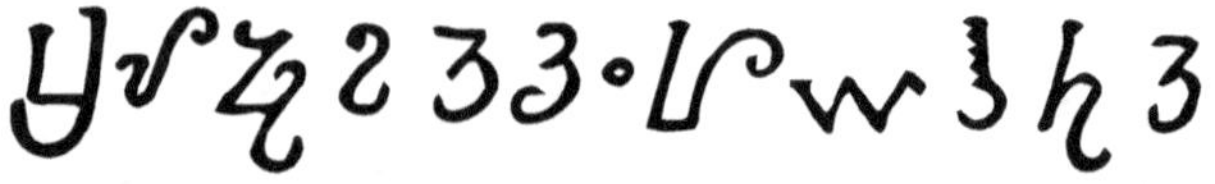

Which being accomplished, recite Psalm II: *Quare fremuerunt gentes et meditati sunt inania.*

Then, make another figure as follows; after which recite Psalm CXV: *Credidi propter quod locutus sum, &c.*

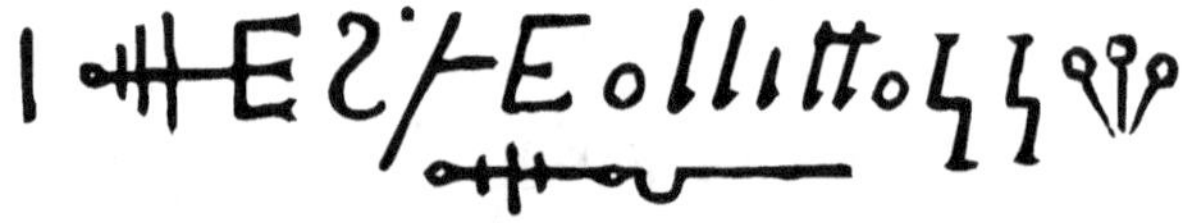

Finally, on the last Monday of the month a Mass for the Dead shall be offered; the Prose shall be omitted, and also the Gospel of St. John, but at the end of the Mass the Priest shall recite the Psalm *Confitemini Domino quoniam bonus, &c.* of which of the four, of Psalm CXV.

†

In Honour of the Most Holy and August Trinity; the Father, the Son, and the Holy Ghost. Amen.

The Seventy-two Sacred Names of God, *Trinitas, Sother, Messias, Emmanuel, Sabahot, Adonay, Athanatos, Jesu, Pentagna, Agragon, Ischiros, Eleyson, Otheos, Tetragrammaton, Ely, Saday, Aquila, magnus Homo, Visio, Flos, Origo, Salvator, Alpha & Omega, Primus, Novissimus, Principium et finis, Primogenitus, Sapientia, Virtus, Paracletus, Via, Veritas, Via, Mediator, Medicus, Salus, Agnus, Ovis, Vitulus, Spes, Aries, Leo, Lux, Imago, Panis, Janua, Petra, Sponsa, Pastor, Propheta, Sacerdos, Sanctus, Immortalis, Jesus-Christus, Pater, Filius hominis, Sanctus, Pater omnipotens Deus, Agios, Resurrectio, Mischiros, Charitas, Æternus, Creator, Redemptor, Unitas, Summum, Bonum, Infinitas,* Amen.

Hereinafter follow the three small pentacles of Solomon, and that of the Gospel of St. John.

Initium sancti Evangelii secundum Joannem, gloria tibi Domini.

In principio erat Verbum, et Verbum erat apud Deum, et Deus erat Verbum. Hoc erat in principio apud Deum. Omnia per ipsum facta sunt: et sine ipso factum est nihil quod factum est. In ipso vita erat, et vita erat lux hominum, et lux in tenebris lucet, et tenebræ eam non comprehenderunt. Fuit homo missus à Deo, cui nomen erat Joannes. Hic venit in testimonium, et testimonium perhiberet de lumine, ut omnes crederent per ipsum. Non erat ille lux, sed ut testimonium perhiberet de lumine. Erat lux vera quæ illuminat omnem hominem venientem in hunc mundum. In mundo erat et mundus per ipsum factus est, et mundus eum non cognovit. In propria venit, et sui

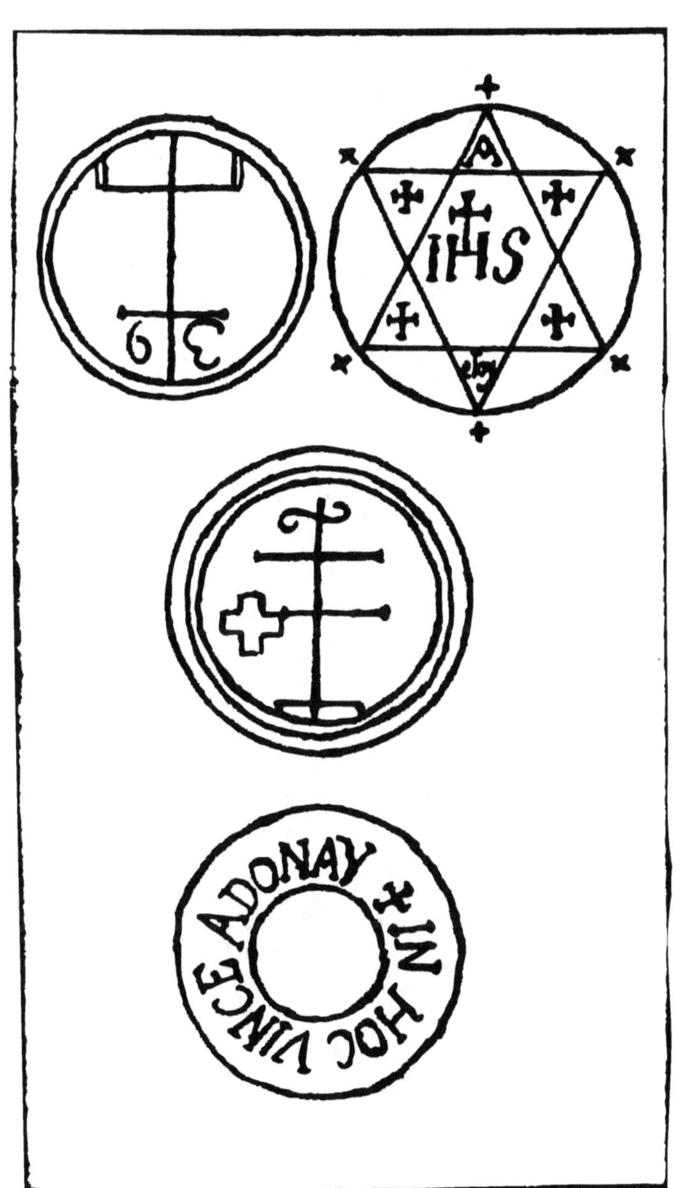

eum non receperunt. Quot quot autem receperunt eum, dedit eis potestatem Filios Dei fieri; his qui credunt in nomine ejus, qui non ex sanquinibus, neque ex voluntate carnis, neque ex voluntate viri, sed ex Deo nati sunt: et Verbum caro factum est, et habitavit in nobis, et vidimus gloriam ejus, gloriam quasi unigenti à Patre plenum gratiæ et veritatis. Deo gratias.

O Zanna Filio David. Benedictus qui venit in nomine Domini, ô zanna in excelsis.

Te invocamus, Te adoramus.

Te laudamus, Te glorificamus.

O Beata et gloriosa Trinitas.

Sit nomen Domini benedictum; ex hoc nunc et usque in seculum. Amen.

✝

In nomine Patris, et Filii, et Spiritus Sancti, Jesus Nazarenus Rex Judæorum. Christus vincit ✝ regnat ✝ imperat ✝ et ab omni malo me defendat. Amen.

Universal Conjuration.

Ego N. conjuro te N. per Deum vivum, per Deum verum, per Deum sanctum et regnantem, qui ex nihilo cœlum et terram et mare, et omnia que in eis sunt, creavit in virtute sanctissimi sacramenti Eucharistiæ et nomine Jesu Christi et potentia ejusdem Filii Dei omnipotentis, qui pro redemptione nostra crucifixus, mortuus et sepultus fuit, et tertia die resurrexit, nuncque sedens ad dexteram psalmatoris totius orbis, inde venturus est judicare vivos et mortuos: et te maledicte incirco per judicem tuum tentare ausus Deus est, te exorciso serpens, tibi qui impero, ut nunc et sine mora appareas mihi juxta circulum pulchra et honesta animæ et corporis formâ, et adimpleas mandata mea sine fallacia aliqua.

Nec restrictione mentali per nomina maxima Dei deorum Domini dominantium Adonay, Tetragrammaton, Jehova, Tetragrammaton, Adonay, Jehova, Otheos, Athanatos, Ischyros, Agla,

Pentagrammaton, Saday, Saday, Saday, Jehova, Otheos, Athanatos, à Liciat, Tetragrammaton, Adonay, Ischyros, Athanatos, Sady, Sady, Sady, Cados, Cados, Cados, Eloy, Agla, Agla, Agla, Adonay, Adonay.

Constringo te pessime et maledicte serpens N. ut sine mora et legione et gravamine in hoc loco libita signa ante circulum meum sine murmure appareas, sine difformitate nec murmur tione iterum.

Exorciso te per nomina Dei ineffabilia Gogmagogque à me pronuntiari non debuerunt et ternoce mea à lapsu venias adsis N. venias adsis N. venias adsis N.

Conjuration.

I, N., do conjure thee, O Spirit N., by the living God, by the true God, by the holy and all-ruling God, who created from nothingness the heaven, the earth, the sea, and all things that are therein, in virtue of the Most Holy Sacrament of the

Eucharist, in the name of Jesus Christ, and by the power of this same Almighty Son of God, who for us and for our redemption was crucified, suffered death, and was buried; who rose again on the third day, and is now seated on the right hand of the Creator of the whole world, from whence he will come to judge the living and the dead; as also by the precious love of the Holy Spirit, perfect Trinity. I conjure thee within the circle, accursed one, by thy judgment, who didst dare to tempt God: I exorcise thee, Serpent, and I command thee to appear forthwith under a beautiful and well-favoured human form of soul and body, and to fulfil my behests without any deceit whatsoever, as also without mental reservation of any kind, by the great times of the God of gods and Lord of lords, Adonay, Tetragrammaton, Jehova, Tetragrammaton, Adonay, Jehova, Otheos, Athanatos, Ischyros, Agla, Pentagrammaton, Saday, Saday, Saday, Jehova, Otheos, Athanatos, à Liciat, Tetragrammaton, Adonay, Ischyros,

Athanatos, Sady, Sady, Sady, Cados, Cados, Cados, Eloy, Agla, Agla, Agla, Adonay, Adonay.

Veni, N. Veni, N. veni, N.

I conjure thee, Evil and Accursed Serpent, N., to appear at my will and pleasure, in this place, before this circle, without tarrying, without companions, without grievance, without noise, deformity, or murmuring. I exorcise thee by the ineffable names of God, to wit, Gog and Magog, which I am unworthy to pronounce; Come hither, Come hither, Come hither. Accomplish my will and desire, without wile or falsehood. Otherwise St. Michael, the invisible Archangel, shall presently blast thee in the utmost depths of hell. Come, then, N., to do my will.

A. P.

Quid tardatis, quid moramini, quid facitis? Preparate vos, obedite præceptori vestro in nomine Domini

Bathat vel Rachat super Abracruens super veniens Abehor super Aberer.

[*Why tarriest thou, and why delayest, what doest thou? Make ready, obey your master, in the name of the Lord, Bathat or Rachat flowing over Abracruens, Abehor or Aberer.*]

L. Q. L. F. A. P.

Behold the Pentacle of Solomon which I have brought into thy presence. I command thee, by order of the great God, Adonay, Tetragrammaton and Jesus. Hasten, fulfil my behests, without wile or falsehood, but in all truth, in the name of the Saviour and Redeemer, Jesus Christ.

Discharge.

Ite in pace ad loca vestra et pax sit inter vos, et vos parati sitis venire vocati. In nomine Patris, et Filii, et Spiritus Sancti. Amen.

THE GRAND PENTACLE
OF SOLOMON.

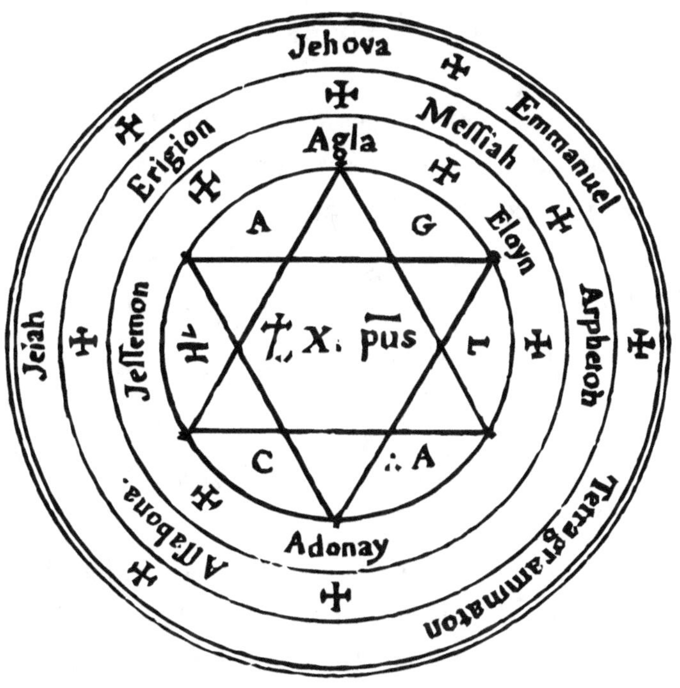

[Go in peace unto your places. May there be peace between us and you, and be ye ready to come when ye are called. In the Name of the Father, and of the Son, and of the Holy Ghost. Amen.]

Act of Thanksgiving.

Laus, honor, gloria et benedictio sit sedenti super thronum et viventi in secula seculorum. Amen.

[Praise, honour, glory, and blessing be unto Him who sitteth upon the throne, who liveth for ever and ever. Amen.]

Conjuration of the Book.

I conjure thee, O Book, to be useful and profitable unto all who shall have recourse to thee for the success of their affairs. I conjure thee anew, by the virtue of the Blood of Jesus Christ, contained daily in the chalice, to be serviceable unto all those who shall read thee. I exorcise thee, in the name of the Most Holy Trinity, in the name of the Most Holy Trinity, in the name of the Most Holy Trinity.

What follows must be said before the sealing of the Book.

I conjure and command you, O Spirits, all and so many as ye are, to accept this Book with good grace, so that whensoever we may read it, the same being approved and recognised as in proper form and valid, you shall be constrained to appear in comely human form when you are called, accordingly as the reader shall judge. In no circumstances shall you make any attempt upon the body, soul, or Spirit of the reader, nor inflict any harm on those who may accompany him, either by mutterings, tempests, noise, scandals, nor yet by lesion or by hindrance in the execution of the commands of this Book. I conjure you to appear immediately when the conjuration is made, to execute without dallying all that is written and enumerated in its proper place in the said book. You shall obey, serve, instruct, impart, and perform all in your power for the benefit of those who command you, and the whole without illusion. If perchance some of the invoked Spirits be unable to come or appear when required, they shall be bound over to send others vested with their power, who also shall swear solemnly to execute all that the reader may demand, and ye are all hereby enjoined by the Most Holy Names of the Omnipotent Living God, Eloym, Jah, El, Eloy, Tetragrammaton, to fulfil everything as it is set forth above. If ye obey me not, I will force you to abide in torments for a thousand years, as also if any one of you receive not this Book with entire resignation to the will of the reader.

Conjuration of the Demons.

In the Name of the Father, and of the Son, and of the Holy Ghost: Take heed. Come, all Spirits. By the virtue and power of your King, and by the seven crowns and chains of your Kings, all Spirits of the Hells are forced to appear in my presence before this pentacle or circle of Solomon, whensoever I shall call them. Come, then, all at my orders, to fulfil that which is in your power, as commanded. Come, therefore, from the East, South, West, and North. I conjure and command you, by the virtue and power of Him who is three, eternal, equal, who is God invisible, consubstantial, in a word, who has created the heavens, the sea, and all which is under heaven.

After these Conjurations you shall command them to affix the Seal.

Concerning the Figure of the Circle.

Circles should be described with charcoal or holy water, sprinkled with the wood of the blessed Cross. When they have been duly made, and the words have been written about the circle, the holy water which has served to bless the same may also be used to prevent the Spirits from inflicting any hurt. Standing in the middle of the circle, you shall command them in a lively manner, as one who is their master.

What must be said in Composing the Circle.

O Lord, we fly to Thy virtue. O Lord, confirm this work. What is operated in us becomes like dust driven before the wind, and the Angel of the Lord pausing, let the darkness disappear, and the Angel of the Lord ever pursuing, Alpha, Omega, Ely, Elohe, Elohim, Zebahot,

Spiritus
Locus
† Et verbum caro factum est, Jesus autem transibat per medium illorum ibat
C. D. P

Elion, Saday. Behold the Lion who is the conqueror of the Tribe of Judah, the root of David. I will open the Book, and the seven seals thereof. I have beheld Satan as a bolt falling from heaven. It is Thou who hast given us power to crush dragons, scorpions, and all Thine enemies beneath Thy feet. Nothing shall harm us, not even Eloy, Elohim, Elohe, Zebahot, Elion, Esarchie, Adonay, Jah, Tetragrammaton, Saday.

The earth and all those who dwell therein belong to God, because He established it upon the seas and prepared it in the midst of the waves. Who shall ascend unto the mountain of the Lord? Who shall be received in his Holy Place? The innocent of hands and clean of heart. Who hath not received his soul in vain, and hath not sworn false witness against his neighbour. The same shall be blessed of God, and shall obtain mercy of God to his salvation. He is of the generation of those who seek Him.

Open your gates, ye princes, open the eternal gates, and the King of Glory shall enter. Who is this King of Glory? The Lord Almighty, the Lord, mighty in battle. Open your gates, ye princes. Lift up the eternal gates. Who is this King of Glory? The Lord Almighty. This Lord is the King of Glory. *Gloria Patri*, &c.

To dismiss them, the Pentacle of Solomon must be exhibited, at the same time saying as follows.

Behold your sentence. Behold that which forbids rebellion to our wills, and doth ordain you to return unto your abodes. May peace be between us and you, and be ready to come back every time you are called to do my will.

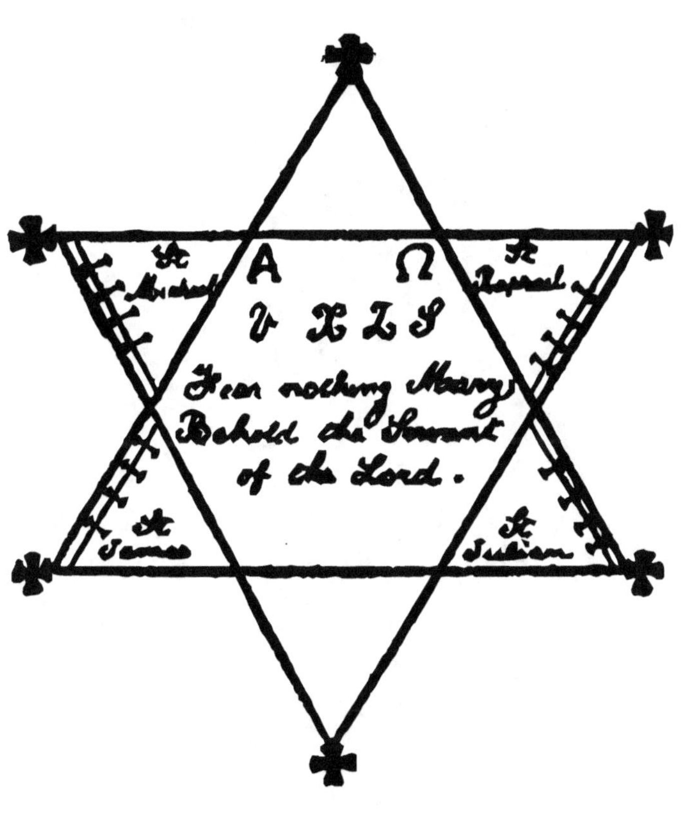
St. Michael
St. Raphael
A
Ω
V X L S
Fear nothing Mary,
Behold the Servant
of the Lord.
St. James
St. Julian

Conjuration of the King of the East.

I conjure and invoke thee, O powerful King of the East MAGOA, by my holy labour, by all the names of Divinity, by the name of the All-Powerful: I command thee to obey, and to come to me, or that failing, forthwith and immediately to send unto me N., currently Masseyel, Asiel, Satiel, Arduel, Acorib, to respond concerning all that I would know and to fulfil all that I shall command. Else thou shalt come verily in thine own person to satisfy my will; which refusing, I shall compel thee by all the virtue and power of God.

The Grand Pentacle or Circle of Solomon will answer for the above and following three Conjurations, which can be said on all days and at all hours. If it be desired to speak only with one Spirit, one only need be named, at the choice of the reader.

Conjuration of the King of the South.

O EGYM, great King of the South, I conjure and invoke thee by the most high and holy Names of God, do thou here manifest, clothed with all thy power; come before this circle, or at least send me forthwith Fadal, Nastraché, to make answer unto me, and to execute all my wishes. If thou failest, I shall force thee by God Himself.

Conjuration of the King of the West.

O BAYEMON, most potent King, who reignest in the Western quarter, I call and I invoke thee in the name of the Divinity. I command thee by virtue of the Most High, to send me immediately before this circle the Spirit N. Passiel, Rosus, with all other Spirits who are subject unto thee, that the same may answer in everything, even as I shall require them. If thou failest, I will

torment thee with the sword of fire divine; I will multiply thy sufferings, and will
burn thee.

Conjuration of the King of the North.

O thou, AMAYMON, King and
Emperor of the Northern parts,
I call, invoke, exorcise, and conjure thee, by the virtue and power of the
Creator, and by the virtue of virtues, to
send me presently, and without delay,
Madael, Laaval, Bamulhae, Belem, Ramat,
with all other Spirits of thine obedience,
in comely and human form. In whatsoever place thou now art, come hither and
render that honour which thou owest to
the true living God, who is thy Creator.
In the name of the Father, of the Son,
and of the Holy Ghost; come therefore,
and be obedient, in front of this circle,
without peril to my body or soul. Appear
in comely human form, with no terror
encompassing thee. I conjure thee, make

haste, come straightway, and at once. By all the Divine names Sechiel, Barachiel; if thou dost not obey promptly, Balandier, suspensus, iracundus, Origratiumgu, Partus, Olemdemis et Bantatis, N., I exorcise thee, do invoke, and do impose most high commandment upon thee, by the omnipotence of the living God, and of the true God; by the virtue of the holy God, and by the power of Him who spoke and all things were made, even by His holy commandment the heaven and earth were made, with all that is in them. I adjure thee by the Father, by the Son, and by the Holy Ghost, even by the Holy Trinity, by that God whom thou canst not resist, under whose empire I will compel thee; I conjure thee by God the Father, by God the Son, by God the Holy Ghost, by the Mother of Jesus Christ, Holy Mother and perpetual Virgin, by her sacred heart, by her blessed milk, which the Son of the Father sucked, by her most holy body and soul, by all the parts and members of this Virgin, by all the sufferings, afflictions,

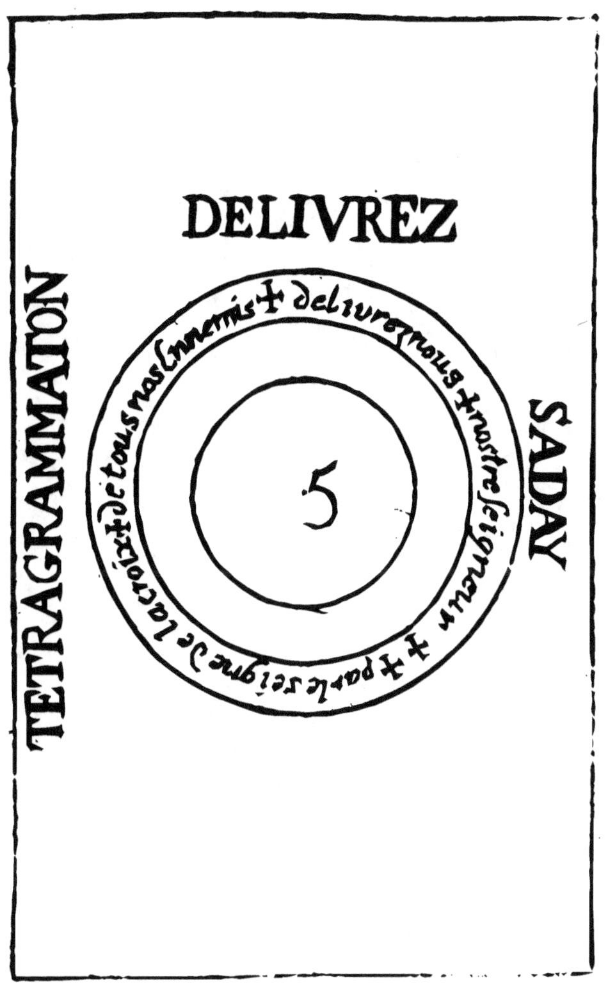

Deliver us † Our Lord †† By the Sign of
the Cross † from all our Enemies †

labours, agonies which she endured during the whole course of her life, by all the sighs she uttered, by the holy tears which she shed whilst her dear Son wept before the time of His dolorous Passion and on the tree of the Cross, by all the sacred holy things which are offered and done, and also by all others, as in heaven so on earth, in honour of Our Saviour Jesus Christ, and of the Blessed Mary, His Mother, by whatsoever is celestial, by the Church Militant, in honour of the Virgin and of all the Saints. In like manner, I conjure thee by the Holy Trinity, by all other mysteries, by the sign of the Cross, by the most precious blood and water which flowed from the side of Jesus Christ, by His Annunciation, and by the sweat which issued from His whole body, when He said in the Garden of Olives: My Father, if it be possible, that these things pass from me, that I may not drink from the chalice of death; I conjure thee by His death and passion, by His burial and glorious resurrection, by His ascension, by the coming of the Holy Ghost. I adjure thee, furthermore, by the crown of thorns which was set upon His head, by the blood which flowed from His feet and hands, by the nails with which He was nailed to the tree of the Cross, by the five holy tears which He shed, by all which He suffered willingly through great love of us: by the lungs, the heart, the hair, the inward parts, and by all the members, of Our Saviour Jesus Christ. I conjure thee by the judgment of the living and the dead, by the Gospel words of Our Saviour Jesus Christ, by His preachings, by His sayings, by all His miracles, by the child in swaddling clothes, by the crying child, borne by the mother in her most pure and virginal womb; by the glorious intercession of the Virgin Mother of Our Saviour Jesus Christ; by all which is of God and of His Most Holy Mother, as in heaven so on earth. I conjure thee by the holy Angels and Archangels, and by all the blessed orders of Spirits, by the holy Patriarchs and Prophets, by all the holy

Martyrs and Confessors, by all the holy Virgins and innocent Widows, and by all the saints of God, both men and women. I conjure thee by the head of St. John the Baptist, by the milk of St. Catherine, and by all the Saints.

CONJURATION FOR EACH DAY OF THE WEEK.

For Monday, to Lucifer. This experience is commonly performed between eleven and twelve, or between three and four. It will take coal, and consecrated chalk to compose the circle, about which these words must be written: I forbid thee, Lucifer, in the name of the Most Holy Trinity, to enter within this circle. A

mouse must be provided to give him; the master must have a stole and holy water, an air also and a surplice. He must recite the Conjuration in a lively manner, commanding sharply and shortly, as a lord should address his servant, with all kinds of menaces: Satan, Rantam, Pallantre, Lutais, Cricacœur, Scircigreur, I require thee to give me very humbly.... &c.

Conjuration of Monday to Lucifer.

I conjure thee, Lucifer, by the living God, by the true God, by the holy God, who spoke and all was made, who commanded and all things were created and made. I conjure thee by the ineffable name of God, On, Alpha & Omega, Eloy, Eloym, Ya, Saday, Lux les Mugiens, Rex, Salus, Adonay, Emmanuel, Messias; and I adjure, conjure, and exorcise thee by the names which are declared under the letters V, 6, X, as also by the names Jehova, Sol, Agla, Rissasoris, Oriston, Orphitue,

Phaton ipreto, Ogia, Speraton, Imagnon, Amul, Penaton, Soter, Tetragrammaton, Eloy, Premoton, Sirmon, Perigaron, Irataton, Plegaton, On, Perchiram, Tiros, Rubiphaton, Simulaton, Perpi, Klarimum, Tremendum, Meray, and by the most high ineffable names of God, Gali, Enga, El, Habdanum, Ingodum, Obu Englabis, do thou make haste to come, or send me N., having a comely and human form in no wise repulsive, that he may answer in real truth whatsoever I shall ask him, being also powerless to hurt me, or any person whomsoever, either in body or soul.

For Tuesday to Frimost.

This experience is performed at night from nine until ten, and the first stone found is given to him. He is to be received with dignity and honour. Proceed as on Monday; compose the circle, and write about it: Obey me, Frimost, obey me, Frimost, obey me, Frimost.

Conjuration.

I conjure and command thee, Frimost, by all the names wherewith thou canst be constrained and bound. I exorcise thee, Nambroth, by thy name, by the virtue of all Spirits, by all characters, by the Jewish, Greek, and Chaldean conjurations, by the confusion and malediction, and I will redouble thy pains and torments from day to day for ever, if thou come not now to accomplish my will and submit to all that I shall command, being powerless to harm me neither in body or soul, nor those in my company.

For Wednesday to Astaroth.

This experience is performed at night, from ten to eleven; it is designed to obtain the good graces of the King and others. Write in the circle as follows: Come, Astaroth, come, Astaroth, come, Astaroth.

Conjuration.

I conjure thee, Astaroth, wicked Spirit, by the words and virtue of God and of Jesus Christ of Nazareth, unto whom all Demons are submitted, who was conceived of the Virgin Mary; by the mystery of the Angel Gabriel, I conjure thee; and again in the name of the Father,

and of the Son, and of the Holy Ghost; in the name of the glorious Virgin Mary, and of the Most Holy Trinity, in whose honour do all the Archangels, Thrones, Dominations, Powers, Patriarchs, Prophets, Apostles, and Evangelists sing without end; Holy, Holy, Holy, Lord God of Hosts, who art, who wast, who art to come, as a river of burning fire. Neglect not my commands, refuse not to come. I command thee by Him who shall appear with flames to judge the living and the dead, unto whom is all honour, praise, and glory. Come, therefore, promptly, obey my will, appear and give praise to the true God, unto the living God, yea, unto all His works; fail not to obey me, and give honour to the Holy Ghost, in whose name I command thee.

For Thursday to Acham.

This experience is made at night, from three to four, at which hour he is called, and appears in the form of a King. A little bread must be given him when he is required to depart; he renders man happy and also discovers treasures. Write about the circle as follows: By the Holy God, by the Holy God, by the Holy God; or another circle within the first, in which will be written: Adonay nasim pin 7. 7. H. M. A.

Conjuration.

I conjure thee, Silcharde, by the image and likeness of Jesus Christ our Saviour, whose death and passion redeemed the entire human race, who also wills that, by His providence, thou appear forthwith in this place. I command thee by all the Kingdoms of God. Act; I adjure and constrain thee by his Holy Name, by Him who walked upon the asp, who crushed the lion and the dragon. Do thou obey me, and fulfil my commands, being powerless to do harm unto me, or any person whomsoever, either in body or soul.

For Friday to Bechard.

This experience is performed at night from eleven to twelve, and a nut must be given to him. Write within the circle: Come, Bechard, come, Bechard, come, Bechard.

Conjuration.

I conjure thee, Bechard, and constrain thee, in like manner, by the Most Holy Names of God, Eloy, Adonay, Eloy, Agla, Samalabactany, which are written in Hebrew, Greek and Latin; by all the sacraments, by all the names written in this book; and by him who drove thee from the height of Heaven. I conjure and com-

mand thee by the virtue of the Most Holy Eucharist, which hath redeemed men from their sins; I conjure thee to come without any delay, to do and perform all my biddings, without any prejudice to my body or soul, without harming my book, or doing injury to those that are in my company.

For Saturday to Guland.

This experience is performed at night from eleven to twelve, and so soon as he appears burnt bread must be given him. Ask him anything you will, and he will obey you immediately. Write in his circle: Enter not, Guland, enter not, Guland, enter not, Guland.

Conjuration.

I conjure thee, O Guland, in the name of Satan, in the name of Beelzebuth, in the name of Astaroth, and in the name of all other Spirits, to make haste and appear before me. Come, then in the name of Satan and in the names of all other Demons. Come to me, I command thee, in the name of the Most Holy Trinity. Come without inflicting any harm upon me, without injury to my body or soul, without maltreating my books, or anything which I use. I command thee to appear without delay, or, that failing, to send me forthwith another Spirit having the same power as thou hast, who shall accomplish my commands and be submitted to my will, wanting which, he whom thou shalt send me, if indeed thou comest not thyself, shall in no wise depart, nor until he hath in all things fulfilled my desire.

For Sunday to Surgat.

This experience is performed at night from eleven to one. He will demand a hair of your head, but give him one of a Fox, and see that he takes it. His office is to discover and transport all treasures, and perform anything that you may will. Write in his circle: Tetragrammaton, 3. Ismael, Adonay, Ilma.

And in a second circle: Come, Surgat, come, Surgat, come, Surgat.

Conjuration.

I conjure thee, Surgat, by all the names which are written in this book, to present thyself here before me, promptly and without delay, being ready to obey me in all things, or, failing this, to dispatch me a Spirit with a stone which shall make me invisible to everyone, whensoever I carry it. And I conjure thee to be submitted in thine own person, or in the

person of him or of those whom thou shalt send me, to do and accomplish my will, and all that I shall command, without harm to me or to any one, so soon as I make known my intent.

Very Powerful Conjuration for all days and hours of the Day or Night, being for Treasures hidden by men or Spirits, that the same may be possessed and transported.

I command you, O all ye Demons dwelling in these parts, or in what part of the world soever ye may be, by whatsoever power may have been given you by God and our holy Angels over this place, and by the powerful Principality of the infernal abysses, as also by all your brethren, both general and special Demons, whether dwelling in the East, West, South, or North, or in any side of the earth, and, in like manner, by the power of God the Father, by the wisdom of God the Son, by the virtue of the Holy Ghost, and by the authority I derive from Our Saviour Jesus Christ, the only Son of the Almighty and the Creator, who made us and all creatures from nothing, who also ordains that you do hereby abdicate all power to guard, habit, and abide in this place; by whom further I constrain and command you, *nolens volens,* without guile or deception, to declare me your names, and to leave me in peaceable possession and rule over this place, of whatsoever legion you be and of whatsoever part of the world; by order of the Most Holy Trinity, and by the merits of the Most Holy and Blessed Virgin, as also of all the saints, I unbind you all, Spirits who abide in this place, and I drive you to the deepest infernal abysses. Thus: Go, all Spirits accursed, who are condemned to the flame eternal which is prepared for you and your companions, if ye be rebellious and disobedient. I conjure you by the same authority, I exhort and call you, I constrain and command you, by all the powers of your superior Demons, to come, obey, and reply positively to what I direct you in the name of Jesus Christ. Whence, if you or they do not obey promptly and without tarrying, I will shortly increase your torments for a thousand years in hell. I constrain you therefore to appear here in comely human shape, by the Most High Names of God, Hain Lon, Hilay, Sabaoth, Helim, Radiaha, Ledieha, Adonay, Jehova, Ya, Tetragrammaton, Saday, Massias, Agios, Ischyros, Emmanuel, Agla, Jesus who is Alpha & Omega, the beginning and the end, that you be justly established in the fire, having no power to reside, habit, or abide in this place henceforth; and I require your doom by the virtue of the said names, to wit, that St. Michael Angel drive you to the uttermost of the infernal abyss, in the name of the Father, and of the Son, and of the Holy Ghost. So be it.

I conjure thee, Acham, or whomsoever thou mayst be, by the Most Holy Names of God, by Malhame, Jac, May, Mabron, Jacob, Desmedias, Eloy, Aterestin, Janastardy, Finis, Agios, Ischyros, Otheos, Athanatos, Agla, Jehova, Homosion, Aja, Messier, Sother, Christus vincit, Christus regnat, Christus imperat, Increatur Spiritus sanctus.

I conjure thee, Cassiel, or whomsoever thou mayest be, by all the said names, with power and with exorcism. I warn thee by the other sacred names of the most great Creator, which are or shall hereafter be communicated to thee; hearken forthwith and immediately to my words, and observe them inviolably, as sentences of the last dreadful day of judgment, which thou must obey inviolately, nor think to repulse me because I am a sinner, for therein shalt thou repulse the commands of the Most High God. Knowest thou not that thou art bereft of thy powers before thy Creator and ours? Think therefore what thou refusest, and pledge therefore thine obedience, swearing by the said last dreadful day of judgment, and by Him who hath created all things by His word, whom all creatures obey. P. *par sedem Baldarcy et per gratiam et diligentem tuam habuisti ab eo hanc nalatimanamilam,* as I command thee.

COLLECTION OF THE RAREST SECRETS
OF THE MAGICAL ART.

To see the Spirits which fill the air.

Take the brain of a rooster, the powder from the grave of a dead man, that is, earth that touches the coffin, walnut oil, virgin wax. Make a composition of the whole, which you will wrap in virgin parchment, in which will be written these two words: GOMERT KAILOETH, with the following character. Burn it all, and you will see prodigious things. But this experiment should be done only by those who fear nothing.

To make three ladies or three gentlemen come in your room, after supper.

Preparation.

For three days it is necessary to abstain from drawing Mercury, and you will be elevated. On the fourth day, as soon as it is morning, clean and prepare your room, as soon as you have dressed, all this time fasting, making sure that your room will not be disturbed for the rest of the day. Note that there shall be nothing hanging or on hooks, like tapestries, clothes, hats, birdcages, curtains, &c. and above all, put clean white sheets on your bed.

Ceremony.

After supper, go secretly to your room, prepared as above. Light a good fire; put a clean white tablecloth on the table, three chairs around, and in front of each place, set a wheat roll and three glasses of clear and fresh water. Then place a chair or seat beside your bed, then go to bed, and say the following words:

Conjuration.

Besticirum confolatio veni ad me vertu Creon, Creon, Creon, cantor Laudem omnipotentis et non commentur. Star superior carta bient Laudem omviestra principiem da montem et inimicos meos ô prostantis vobis et mihi dantes quo passium fieri sui cisibilis.

The three persons having arrived, will sit near the fire, drinking, eating and then will thank the one who received them: because if a woman performs this ceremony, three gentlemen will come; and if it is a man, there will come three young ladies. These three people will draw lots among themselves to see who will stay with you: she will sit in the seat or chair that you have provided for them, next to your bed, and she will stay chatting with you until midnight; and at this time, she will go with her companions, without there being any need to send them away. As for the other two, they will stand by the fire while the other talks to you; and while she is with you, you can question her about such art or science, and anything that you wish; she will immediately give you a positive answer. You can also ask her if she knows of any hidden treasure, and she will tell you the place and the convenient time to raise it, and will even be there with her companions to defend you against the attacks of the infernal spirits who could have possession of it; and leaving from you, she will give you a ring, which will make you lucky in gambling by wearing it on your finger; and if you put it on the finger of a woman or young girl, you will enjoy her immediately.

Nota.——That you must leave the window open so that she can come in. You can repeat this same ceremony as often as you wish.

To make a girl come to you, however modest she may be. Experiment of a marvellous power of the superior intelligences.

It should be observed, from the first quarter to the waning of the moon, a very bright star between eleven and midnight; but before beginning do as follows.

Take a virgin parchment, on which you will write the name of the person whom you desire to come. The parchment must be cut in the manner shown on the first line of the following figure.

The two NN indicates the place for the names. On the other side of the parchment, write these words: *Machidael Bareschas*; then put the parchment on the earth, the names against the ground, your right foot on it and your left knee on the ground. Holding in the right hand a white wax candle that can last for an hour, look at the brightest star and say the following conjuration.

Conjuration.

I salute thee and conjure thee, O beautiful Moon and beautiful Star, as well as the bright light which I hold in my hand, by the air that is within me, and by the earth that I am touching. I conjure thee, by all the names of the Spirit princes that presides in you, by the ineffable name ON, which created everything, by you, beautiful angel Gabriel with Prince Mercury, Michael and Melchidael. I conjure thee again, by all the Names of God, that you send to possess, torment, harass the body, the soul and the five senses of N., whose name is written on this parchment, so that she comes to me and fulfills my will, that she has no friendship for anyone in the world, especially for N. as long as she is indifferent towards me. May she cannot endure. May she be obsessed, suffer and tormented. Go, therefore, promptly Melchidael, Bareschas, Zazel, Tiriel, Malcha and all those who are under your command. I conjure thee, by the great liv-

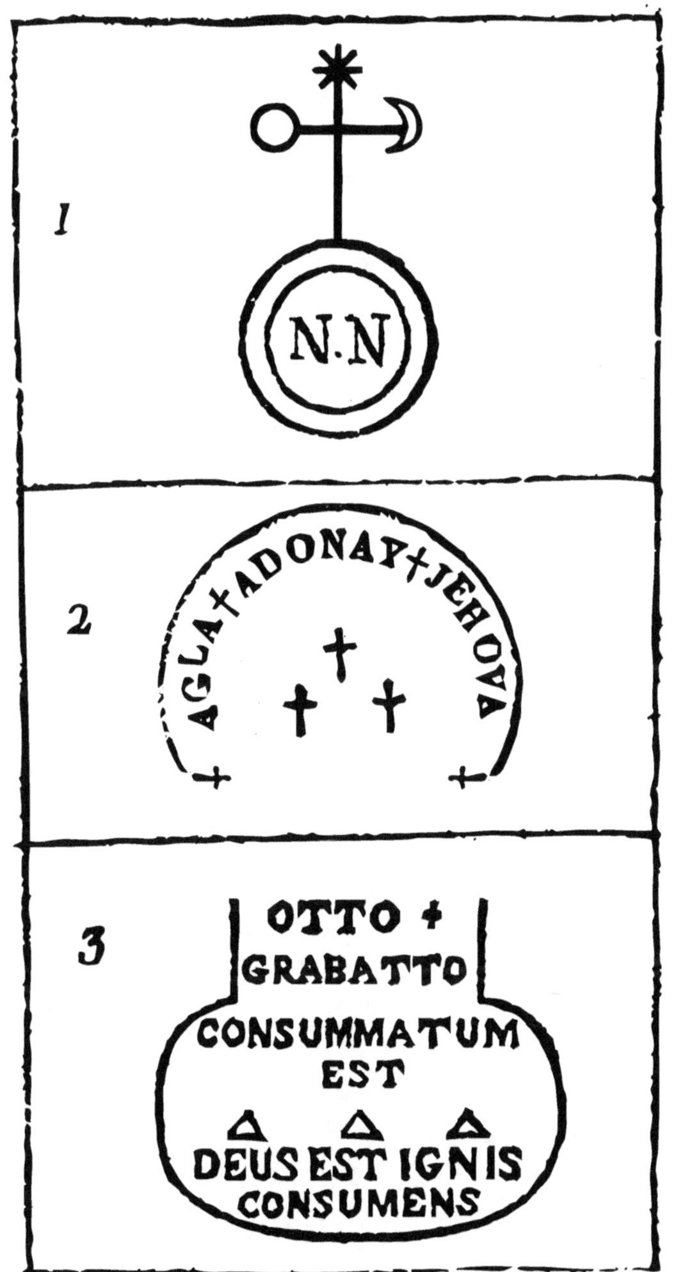
1
N.N
2
AGLA✝ADONAY✝JEHOVA
3
OTTO ✝ GRABATTO
CONSUMMATUM EST
DEUS EST IGNIS CONSUMENS

ing God, to send her speedily to satisfy my will. Me N., I promise to satisfy you.

Having repeated this conjuration three times, put the candle on the parchment and let it burn. The next day, take said parchment and put it in your left shoe. You leave it there until the person whom you have made this operation comes to find you. It is necessary, in the conjuration, specify the day you want her to come and she will not be absent.

To win at games.

Gather the herb called *Morsus Diaboli* on the eve of St. Peter, before sunrise. Put it on the blessed stone for a day, then dry it, powder it and carry it with you. To pick it, you have to make this semicircle, with the names and crosses marked on the second line of the above plate.

To put out a fire in a fireplace.

Make on the fireplace, with a coal, the characters and words of the above plate, third line, and three times pronounce the words: In hoc Vince Adonay.

To make oneself invisible.

Begin this operation on a Wednesday, before sunrise, being provided with seven black beans, then we take a human skull. Put a bean in the mouth, two others in the nostrils, two others in the eyes, and two in the ears. Next, make on this head the character here shown, then bury the said head with the face towards the sky.

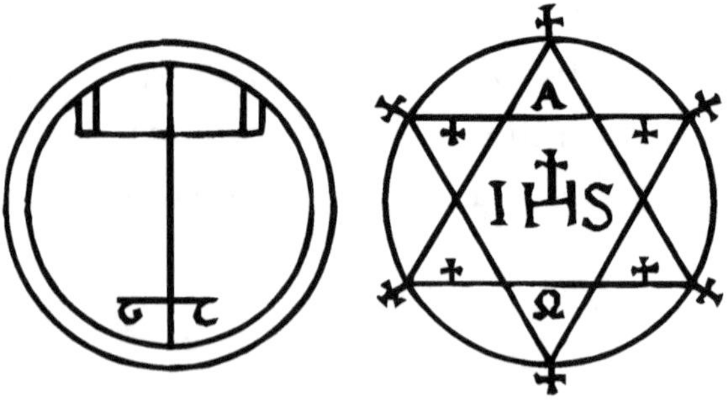

Water it for nine days with excellent brandy, in the morning when the sun is up. On the eighth day, you will find the deferred Spirit there, who will ask you, "What are you doing there?" You will answer him, "I am watering my plant." He will tell you, "Give me this bottle, I will water it myself." You will tell him that you do not want to. He will ask you again, but you must continue to refuse until he stretches out his hand, and there you will see in it the figure similar to the one you made on the head, which will hang from the tips of his fingers. In this case, you must be assured that it is indeed the true Spirit of the head: because someone else could surprise you, causing harm to you and your operation would become unsuccessful.

When you have given your flask, he will water it himself and you will take you leave. The next day, which is the ninth day, you will return there; you will find your ripe beans. You will take them; you will put one in your mouth, then you will look in a mirror; if you don't see yourself, it will be good. You will do the same to all the others; or testing them in the mouth of a child. All those which will be worth nothing must be buried where the head is.

To have Gold and Silver, or the Hand of Glory.

Pull out the hair, with its root, from a mare in heat, closest to the nature, saying: Dragne, Dragne. Secure the hair, and immediately buy a new earth pot with the cover, without haggling. Return home; fill this pot with water from a spring, up to two fingers near the edge. Place the said hair into the pot, which you must cover. Put it in a place where it cannot be seen by either you or others, because there would be danger.

After a period of nine days, and at the same time that you hid it, go uncover it; you will discover inside a small animal in the shape of a snake. He will stand up-

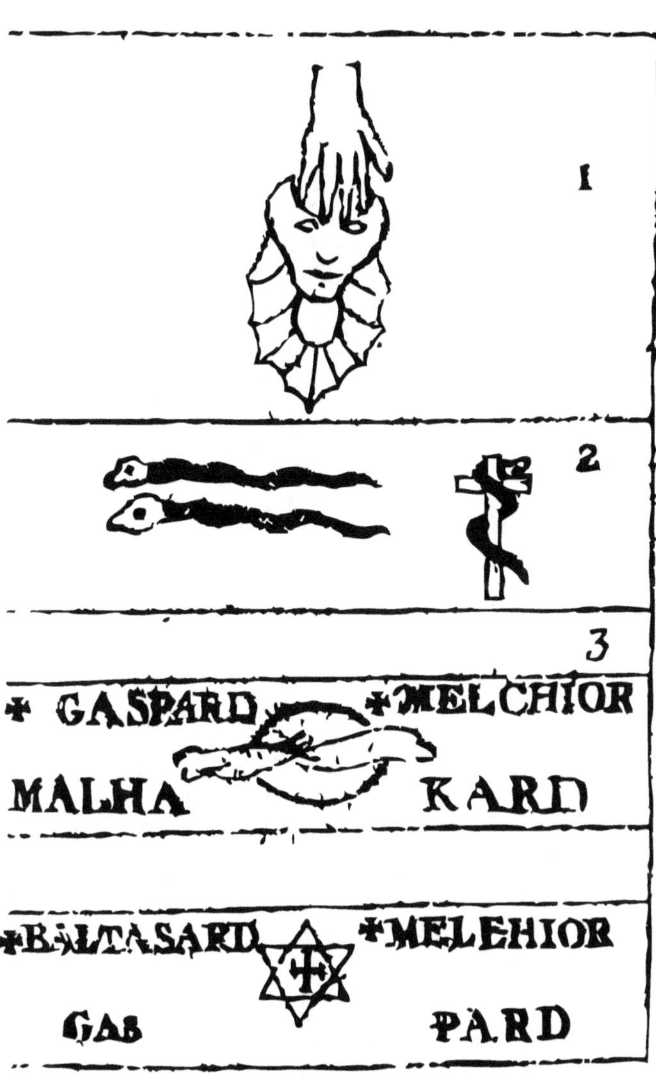
1
2
3
+ GASPARD   + MELCHIOR
MALHA   KARD
+ BALTASARD   + MELEHIOR
GAS   PARD

right; you will tell him immediately, "I accept the pact." This done, you will take it without touching it with your hand; you will put it in a new box bought expressly for the purpose without haggling: you will put wheat bran in it, nothing else; but you must not fail to give it to him every day; and when you want to have silver or gold, you will put in the box as much as you want to have, and you will lie down on your bed, putting your box near you, and sleep, if you want, for three or four hours. After this time, you will find double the money you put in; but you must be careful to put the same one back.

Note that the small figure, second line, only comes by the force of the charm; so you cannot put more than 100 pounds at a time. But if, however, your planet gives you dominance over supernatural things, the serpent will be in the likeness of the second figure of the same line as above; that is to say, he will have a face approaching the human face, and you will be able to put up to 1000 pounds; every day you will get twice as much. If we wanted to get rid of it, we can give it to whoever we want, provided that they accept it, putting the figure we have with a cross, to the line made on virgin parchment in the box, or, instead of the ordinary wheat that is commonly given, you will have to give him bran from the flour from which a Priest will have said his first Mass, and he will die; above all, do not forget any circumstance, because there is no mockery in this matter.

Garters for travelling.

Leave your house on an empty stomach, walk to your left until you find a merchant selling ribbons. Buy a yard of white one; pay whatever is asked of you, and drop a liard in the shop, return home by the same route. The next day, do the same until you find a merchant selling feathers. Buy one cut, just as you bought the ribbon; and when you are back in your dwelling, write with your own blood on the ribbon, the characters of the third line, it is the white right garter above; those of the fourth are for the left. When this is done, leave your house; on the third day, wear your ribbon and your quill; walk left until you find a pastry chef or a baker; buy a cake or a loaf of bread for two liards; go to the first tavern, order a half-bottle of wine, have the glass rinsed three times by the same person, break the cake or bread into three pieces; put the three pieces in the glass with the wine. Take the first piece and toss it under the table, without looking there, saying: "Irly, for you." Then take the second piece and toss it away, saying: "Terly, for you." Write on the other side of the garter the names of these two Spirits with your blood; toss away the third piece, saying: "Eirly, for you." Throw away the quill, drink the wine without eating, pay your due and leave. Being out of town, put on your garters; be careful not to mistakenly put the one that is for the right on the left, there is consequence. Stamp your foot three times on the ground, calling out the names of the Spirits: Irly, Terly, Erly, Balthazar, Melchior, Gaspard, let us walk. Then make your journey.

To be hard against all kinds of weapons.

Take Easter holy water and some wheat flower; make a paste of these, and find yourself at the death of someone who dies a violent death, such as of a hanged man, or other justice. Get as close to him as you can, and without saying anything, take out your dough. Then, when you feel that he is passing, conjure his Spirit to come and lock himself into your dough, to defend you against all kinds of weapons. Return home, and make little dough balls; twist them in virgin parchment, where the following is written: 1. u, n., 1. a. Fau, 1. Moot, and Dorhort. Amen. You have to swallow these balls.

It is necessary to say, when making the balls, five times *Pater*, and five times *Ave*, etc.

Nota.—That the number of these balls is arbitrary, and that the preceding characters are written on a single piece of virgin parchment, which we divide into as many parts as we make balls. It is necessary to say the baptismal name of the patient in the conjuration.

Conjuration to the Sun.

Take a paper, make a hole in it, look through it towards the rising sun, saying: I conjure you, Solar Spirit, on behalf of the great living God, that you may show me N.; then continue like this: *anima mea turbata est valde; sed tu, Domine, usquequo*; repeat three times.

To make a person come.

Fagot burns the heart, the body, the soul, the blood, the spirit, the understanding of N. by fire, by the sky, by the earth, by the rainbow, by Mars, Mercury, Venus, Jupiter, Feppé, Feppé, Feppé, Elera, and in the name of all the Devils, Fago, possesses, burns the heart, the body, the soul, the blood, the spirit, the understanding of N. until may he come and fulfill all my desires and wishes. Go in lightning and ashes, and in storm, Santos, Quisor, Carracos, Arné, Tourne, that he cannot sleep, nor remain in place, nor do, nor eat, nor river to cross, nor horse to ride; neither man, nor woman, nor girl speak until he comes to fulfill all my desires and wishes.

To make a girl dance nude.

On virgin parchment, write the first character of the following figure, with the blood of a bat. Then place it on a blessed stone so that a Mass is said on it. After which, when you want to use it, place this occult character under the threshold of the door where the person you are thinking of must pass. As soon as she has passed by, you will see her burst into fury, taking off her clothes and stripping herself completely naked. If you do not remove the character, she will dance until she dies, making grimaces and contortions which will cause more pity than desire.

To see at night in a vision, what you wish to know about the past or future.

The two N.N. which you see in the small circle of the present second figure, shows the place where you must write your name. And to know what you desire, write the names that are in the circle on virgin parchment, being done before sleeping, and put it on your right ear, while retiring, saying the following orison three times.

Orison.

In the glorious name of the great living God, to whom, in all times, all things are present to him, I who am your servant N., Eternal Father, I beg you to send me your Angels who are written in this circle, and that they show me what I am curious to know and learn, by Our Saviour Jesus Christ. So be it.

When your orison is finished, lie down on your right side, and you will see in a dream what you desire.

For nailing or make a person suffer.

Go to a cemetery, collect nails from an old coffin, saying: "Nails, I take you so that you can help me to divert and hurt anyone I want; in the name of the Father, the Son and the Holy Spirit. Amen."

When you want to use it, you will find a footprint, and make the third figures as shown on the plate. Drive the nail in the middle, saying, *Pater noster*, until *in terra*. Hit the nail with a stone, saying: "May you hurt N. until I pull you out of there." Cover the area with a little dust and note it well; for you cannot cure the evil that it causes except by pulling the nail out while saying: "I remove you, so that the harm you have caused to N. ceases; in the name of the Father, the Son and the Holy Spirit. Amen." Then pull out the nail and erase the characters, not with the same hand you made them, but with the other; because there would be danger for the maleficent.

To prevent a person from sleeping all night, and to ensure that he does not rest until he has spoken to you, even though he wished you mortal harm, and was far away from you.

The night you want to operate this secret, be the last one in the house to go to retire for the night; before going to bed, you will have prepared a fire in the hearth, and particularly that there is good wood lighted stick. Being against the chimney, put the palm of your left hand in a place of the chimney that it is black and smoked, holding it closed and open, you will say these words seven times, "*Cinque furono li appicati, linque, linque furono li tana liati vi scongiro per Béelzebut che linque vi fate ache date a tormentar il cuore et le visuere* (of such and such N.) for my love. Amen."

After having repeated them seven times, thrust the stick well into the embers, and with the hand beat three times against the black of the fireplace, cover your fire with ashes, and you go to bed. You will

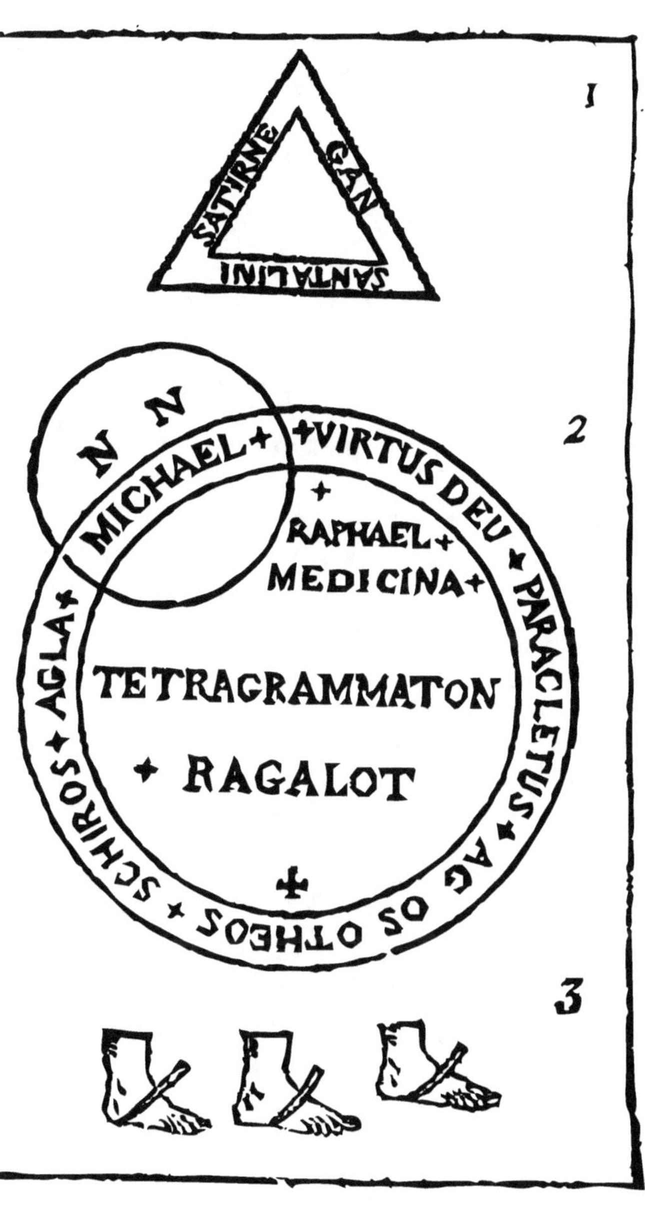

1

SATIRNE
GAN
SANTALINI

2

N N
MICHAEL
VIRTUS DEU
RAPHAEL
MEDICINA
PARACLETUS
AGLA
TETRAGRAMMATON
RAGALOT
AG
SCHIROS
OS OTHEOS

3

see that the one for whom you have done this will not be able to live or last until he has given you satisfaction with what you desire. This is one of the rare secrets that Necromancy has invented.

To seem to be accompanied by many.

Take a handful of sand, and conjure it thus: Anachi, Jehova, Hælersa, Azarbel, rets caras sapor aye pora caco-tamo lopidon ardagal margas poston eulia buget Kephar, Solzeth Karne phaca ghedolos salesetata.

Place the sand thus conjured into an ivory box with the powdered skin of a tiger snake. Then throw it into the air while reciting the conjuration and there will appear as many men as there are grains of sand; do this on the day and at the hour when the sun is in the Sign of Mary, the Virgin.

To not be wounded by any weapon.

Recite every morning: "I rise in the name of Jesus Christ who has been crucified for me: May Jesus bless me; may Jesus wants to lead me; may Jesus guard me; may Jesus desires to govern and lead me to eternal life, in the name of the Father, and of the Son, and of the Holy Ghost." It should be said three times before retiring to bed and before rising. The following will be written on the sword or weapon you wish to use: Ibel, Ebel, Abel.

To enjoy who you want. Secret of Father Girard.

Be three days without extracting mercury that before swallowing nutmeg; on the fourth day, while fasting, you will say; "To God, the *torum cultin, cultorum, bultin bultotum,* come close to me, my companion." You have to swallow the nutmeg, saying: "Come close, &c." Once you have done this, when you take a leak, do not bother with the nutmeg. This secret serves for the whole life without having to repeat it. You only have to say the last three words while blowing in the face, or by kissing everyone you want to be loved.

To make a weapon fail.

Take a new clay pipe, fitted with its brass cap, fill it with powdered Mandrake root, then blow through the pipe while silently pronouncing to yourself : "*Abla, Got, Bata, Bata, Bleu.*"

Against pleurisy.

Infuse on a sand bath, for two hours ; in a pint of good white wine, ten to twelve pieces of new droppings either from horse, donkey or mule. Having poured and squeezed out this liquor while still hot, pour it into a glass at the bottom of which you will have written before-hand, *Dia, Bix, On, Dabulh, Cherih.* Drink it in a well-covered bed, and the next day you will be healed.

Against fevers.

Dissolve half an ounce of green Rosacea in a glass of water; write with this dissolution on a slip of paper, the size of your thumb, the words: *Agla, Garnaze, Eglatus, Egla.* Swallow such a note five days in a row. During these five days, take the following preparations:

For intermittent fever.

Before the attack, take a dram of pow-dered great Gentian root.

For tertiary fever.

Apply to your navel, the root of Dog's tongue newly dug from the ground, cleaned and cut into slices, with a cloth on top to hold it there, renew it every twelve hours.

For quartan fever.

At the beginning of the attack take a dram of Myrrh in a glass of white wine; repeat three times.

To stop blood loss.

Write with blood, INRI on a piece of paper which you will apply to the forehead. You will then use the powder that comes out of the cavity of the dried fruit of the plant called wolf puffball, mixed with egg white; if the loss takes place internally, such as spitting and vomiting of blood, put alum powder in a preserved of red rose, eat it in the morning on an empty stomach and in the evening when going to bed, until cured.

Against a sword strike.

Before going to fight, write on a ribbon of any colour the following two words: *Buoni jacum, I have nothing to do with you.* Tighten your right wrist with this ribbon; fear not, defend yourself, and the sword of your enemy will never touch you.

For when going to an action.

Say five *Pater* and five *Ave* in honour of the five wounds of Our Saviour. Then say three times, "I am going in the shirt of Notre-Dame; may I be enveloped by the wounds of my God, by the four crowns of heaven, by Mr. St John the Evangelist, St Luke, St Matthew and St Mark; may they guard me; may no man, woman nor lead, neither iron nor steel, wound me, cut me, nor crush my bones, for the peace of God."

And when we have said the above, you have to swallow the following words: *Est *principio, est in principio, est in verbum, Deum et tu phantu.* It is for twenty-four hours.

To extinguish fire.

Say, "Great ardent fire, I conjure thee by the Great Living God, to lose thy colour as did Judas, when he betrayed our Lord on the day of Good Friday. In the Name of the Father, and of the Son, and of the Holy Ghost." It is to be repeated three times, while giving a kick or a punch, and we throw into the fire as much cut and soaked hay as can be procured.

Against burns.

Fire, lose thy heat, as Judas did lose his colour, when he betrayed our Saviour in the Garden of Olives. This is to be pronounced three times over the burn, blowing on it each time.

Then wrap the burn with a thick wad of cotton wool placed, or put compresses of strong wine vinegar on it, which you will change every two hours on the first day; and every six hours on the following days.

Against headaches.

Take some powdered black pepper, mix it with some good brandy to make a kind of slurry out of it. Shape a headband with it, which you will apply on the forehead while pronouncing the words, three times, "*Millant, Vah, Vitalot.*" Then say three *Pater.*

Against flux.

You must drink, while fasting, three days in a row, four ounces of purified plantain juice, and say each time the following:

"I have entered into the Garden of Olives, I have met Saint-Elizabeth, she told me about the flux of her stomach, I asked her to grace mine; and she ordered me to say *Pater* three times in honour of God, and *Ave* three times in honour of M. St Jean." Say three *Pater* and three *Ave*, as it is said above and you will be healed.

To prevent from eating at the table.

Nail under the table a needle that has been used to bury a dead man, and which had pierced his flesh, then say, "*Coridal, Nardac, Degon.*" Then you will place a piece of Assa fœtida onto burning charcoal, and take your leave.

To extinguish fire.

Instead of the words indicated before for the same thing, say the following, after making the sign of the cross: "*Anania,*

Anassia, Emisael, libera nos Domine." Then throw away the cut and soaked straw as mentioned.

To prevent copulation.

For this experiment, you must have a new penknife, then, on a Saturday, at the precise time of Moon rise, while it is waning, you will trace with the point, behind the door of the room where the people sleep, the following characters as well as the words, *Consummatum est*, and break the point of the penknife in the door.

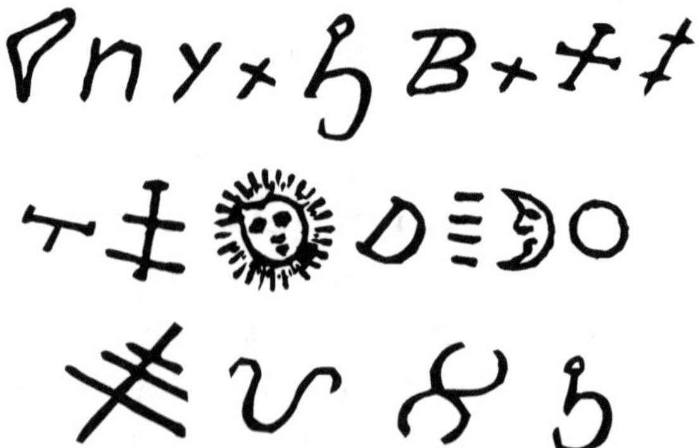

For Games.

During stormy weather, gather some four or five leaf clover, making over them the sign of the cross, then say: "Trifle or large clover, I pick you in the name of the Father, and of the Son, and of the Holy Ghost, by the virginity of the Holy Virgin, by the virginity of St John the Baptist, by the virginity of St John the Evangelist, that you may serve me in all kinds of games." You have to say five *Pater* and five *Ave*, then continue, "*El, Agios, Ischyros, Athanatos.*" You will keep this clover in a black silk bag that you will wear like a scapular each time that you play. At other times, take care to put it in a safe place.

To stop a Snake.

Throw after it, a piece of paper dipped in a solution of alum, and on which you have written with the blood of a kid goat: "Stop, fair one, here's a forfeit." Then whistle a wicker rod in front of it: if it is touched with this rod, it will die immediately, otherwise it will promptly flee.

To prevent a Dog from biting or barking.

Say three times, looking at the dog, "The barbaric bow, the heart splits, the tail hangs, the key of St Peter closes your mouth until tomorrow."

Against ringworm.

Say for ten days the following: "Saint Peter on the bridge of God sat down; Our Lady of Caly came there and said to him: Peter, what are you doing here? Lady, it is on account of the hurt of my master that I placed myself here. St Peter, you will get up; to St Ager you will go; you will take some holy ointment from the mortal wounds of Our Lord; you will grease yourself with it, you will say three times; *Jesus, Maria,* and you will make the sign of the cross on your head three times." After these words, apply each time, on the head, a hot poultice of watercress fricassee with pork fat.

For game of dices.

Dice, I conjure you in the name of Assizer and of Rassize, that they may come raid and grab in the names of Assia and Longrio. Note that you must wear the scapular made of clover leaves, as mentioned earlier.

To remove a fish-bone from the throat.

We use a medium-sized leek from which the roots or filaments have been removed. For this purpose, we dip it in salad oil, and we insert it into the gullet several times, if necessary, pronouncing these words: *"Blaise, martyr and servant of Jesus Christ, I command you to go up or downward."*

To walk without being tired.

Write on three silk ribbons, *Gaspard, Melchior, Balthazar.* Tie one of these ribbons above the right knee, without tightening it; the second above the left knee, and the third around the kidneys. Before setting out, swallow a small glass of anise in some broth or in a glass of white wine, and rub your feet with rhue crushed in olive oil.

To win at all games.

We have already made known several ways to win at games, here is another that we have found in an old manuscript, we have not yet been able to judge its merit.

Write on virgin parchment the following words and crosses: † Ibel † Laber
† Chabel † Habet † Rabel. You have to
carry it with you.

To avoid suffering at the question.

Swallow a slip of paper where the
following is written in your own
blood; Aglas, Aglanos, Algadenas,
Imperiequeritis, *tria pendent corpora tamis dis
meus et gestas in medio et divina potestas dimeas
clamator, sed jestas ad astra levatur*, or again:
Tel, Bel, Quel, Caro, Mon, Aqua.

Secrets and counter-charms, by Guidon, Practitioner in occult healings.

The secrets that follow are as sure
as they are infallible. Guidon, who
practises them daily, has carried out cures,
by means of them, which prove that we
are in no position to be able to question

them. The whole country of Caux and Normandy are convinced of this. He carries out his experiments in public as well as in private; guided by a zeal of charity, he undertakes, with the same courage, the poor as the wealthy; by this means, he acquired the esteem and protection of those respectable people he knew; he works tirelessly for magical destruction, and looks with horror at the evil perpetrators.

Operation from Guidon, when it comes to dispossession.

The ancient rituals are of great resources to him, he omits neither Conjurations, Exorcisms, Gospels, nor Prayers; he only removes, for irrational animals, the places where dead people are spoken of with the signs of the Cross; he uses holy water, most often baptismal water, which he sprinkles in the shape of a cross on the fanatic, with a branch of blessed boxwood; he also signs the cursed person on the forehead with his thumb dipped in the same water. During the ceremony, he is bareheaded, as are the victim and the assistants. When he operates on irrational animals, instead of holy water, he throws prepared salt, as we will say. He continues his operation with the Orison of the Enchiridion, printed in Rome in 1660, p. 43; then he takes salt in a bowl, which he exorcises with blood taken from one of the cursed animals; he stirs everything, saying: *"Beati tornitis omnes Joannes Baptisantes et agentes."*

He then makes a novena at home, which is to recite, for nine days while fasting, the Orison from the Enchiridion as mentioned.

To lift and destroy all curses.

Take a cup of salt, more or less, depending on the quantity of the cursed animals; pronounce on it the following:

"Herego gomet hunc gueridans sesserant de-liberant amei."

Make three circles around the animals, starting at the side of the rising sun, and continuing following the course of this star, the animals in front of you, and making your jets on them by pinch, reciting the same words.

The great Exorcism to dispossess either the human creature, or unreasonable animals.

Demon, leave the body of N., by the command of the God whom I adore, and yield for the Holy Spirit. I place the sign of the Holy Cross of Our Lord Jesus Christ on your forehead. In the name of the Father, and of the Son, and of the Holy Spirit. I make the sign of the Cross of Our Lord Jesus Christ over your breast. In the name of the Father, and of the Son, and of the Holy Spirit. Eternal and Almighty God, Father of Our Lord

Jesus Christ, cast the eyes of your mercy upon your servant N. whom you have deigned to call to the right hand of faith, heal his heart of all manner of elements and misfortunes, and break all his chains and bonds. Lord, open the door of your glory by your goodness, so that, being marked with the seal of your wisdom, he may be free from the stench, attacks and desires of the foul Spirit; and being filled with the sweet odour of your bounties and graces, he joyfully observes your commandments in your Church; and advancing day by day in perfection, he is made worthy of having received the salutary remedy for his faults, through your holy Baptism, by the merits of the same Jesus Christ Our Lord and God. Lord, we beseech you to answer our prayers, to preserve and protect what a charitable love has made you redeem at the price of your precious blood, and by the virtue of your Holy Cross, by which we are marked. Jesus, protector of the poor and afflicted, be favourable unto the people you have adopted, making us partakers of the New Testament, so that the letters of promise may be fulfilled and received by your grace what they can only hope for through you, Jesus Christ Our Saviour, who is our recourse, who made Heaven and Earth. I exorcise you, creature, in the name of God, the Father Almighty, and by the love that Our Christ Jesus bears, and by the virtue of the Holy Spirit; I exorcise you by the great living God, who is the true God that I adore, and by the God who created you, who has preserved all his chosen ones, who has commanded his servants to bless him, for the benefit of those who believe in him, so that everything becomes a salutary Sacrament to drive out the enemy. It is for this reason, Lord our God, that we beseech you to sanctify this salt with your holy benediction, and to make it a perfect remedy for those who receive it. May it remain in their bowels, so that they may be incorruptible, in the name of Our Lord Jesus Christ, who is to judge the Quick and the Dead, and by the seal of the God of Abraham, the God of Isaac, the God of Jacob, the God who was appeared to his servant Moses on Mount Sinai, who drew the children of Israel out of Egypt, giving them an Angel to protect them and lead them day and night. I also beseech you, Lord, to send your holy Angel to protect your servant N. and lead him to eternal life, in virtue of your holy Baptism. I exorcise you, impure and rebellious Spirit, in the name of God the Father, God the Son, God the Holy Spirit; I command you to leave the body of N., I adjure you to withdraw in the name of the One who gave Saint Peter his hand when he was about to drown into the water. Obey your God, cursed Demon, and obey the sentence pronounced against you, and honour the living God, honour the Holy Spirit and Jesus Christ, sole-begotten Son of the Father. Be gone, ancient serpent, from the body of N. for the great God commands you to do so; let your pride be confounded and annihilated before the sign of the Holy Cross, with which we have been marked by the baptism and grace of Jesus Christ. Consider that the day of your torment approaches, and that unbearable torments await you; that your judgment is irrevocable, that your sentence condemns you and all your companions to eternal flames, on account of your rebellion against your Creator. Therefore, accursed Demon, I command you to flee for the sake of God, whom I adore; flee by the Holy God, by the True God, by Him who said, and all was done: render honour to the Father, the Son and the Holy Spirit, and to the most holy and indivisible Trinity. I command you, unclean Spirit, whosoever you may be, to leave the body of this creature N. created by God, who is the same God, Our Saviour Jesus Christ, that today he may deign by his infinite bounty, to call you to the grace of partaking in his holy Sacraments which he has instituted for the salvation of all the faithful. In the name of God, who will judge the whole world by fire.

Behold the cross of Our Saviour Jesus Christ. † Flee, opposing parties, behold the lion of the tribe of Judah, root of David.

To lift all Spells, and bring in the person who caused the harm.

Take the heart of one of the dead animals; making sure there is no sign of life. Tear out the heart, put it on a clean plate, then have nine hawthorn needles, and proceed as follows.

Pierce the heart with one of your needles, saying: "Adibaga, Sabaoth, Adonay, *contra ratout prisons pererunt fini unixio paracle gossum.*"

Take two of your needles and pierce, saying: *"Qui fussum mediator agros gaviol valax."*

Take two more, and while piercing, say: *"Landa zazar valoi sator salu xio paracle gossum."*

Take again two of your needles, and while piercing, say: *"Mortus cum fice sunt et per flagellationem Domini nostri Jesu-Christi."*

Finally, pierce using the last two needles with the following words: *"Avir sunt* devant vous *paracletur strator verbonum offisum fidando."*

Then continue, saying:

"I call upon those, men or women, who have had the Missal of Abel made; coward, it was done wrong that leaving to come find us by sea or by land, from everywhere, without delay and without disdain."

Pierce then the heart with a nail to these last words.

Note that if you cannot get hawthorn needles, you will use new nails.

Once the heart has been pierced, as described above, place it in a small bag and hang it from the chimney. The next day, take the heart out of the bag, put it on a plate, removing the first needle you will pierce it anew in another place of the heart, saying the intended words above.

You will remove two more; and piercing them again, will say the appropriate words. Finally, you will remove them all in the same order to pierce them again as before, observing never to pierce in the same hole twice. Continue this experiment for nine days. However, if you don't want to give any rest to the evildoer, do your novena on the same day, and in the order prescribed in the last operation.

Pierce the heart with the nail, uttering the intended words for this purpose, then build a large fire; put the heart on a grill, to roast it on the glowing embers. The evildoer must come to beg for mercy. Otherwise if it is out of his power to come within the short time you grant him, you will cause him to die.

The Castle of Belle.
Guard for the Horses.

Take some salt on a plate; then having your back against the sunrise, and with the animals before you, pronounce the following, being on your knees, bareheaded:

"Salt which is made and formed at the Castle of Belle Saint Belle Elisabeth, in the name of Disolet, Solfée carrying salt, salt whose salt, I conjure you in the name of Gloria, of Doriante and Galianne her sister; salt I conjure you that you keep hold for me my lively horses of equine beasts who are present before God and before me, healthy and clean, drinking well, eating well, large and fat, that they may be at my will; salt whose salt, I conjure you by the power of glory, and by the virtue of glory, and in all my intention always of glory."

This being pronounced in the corner of the rising sun, go to the other corner following the course of this star, and there you will pronounce the above. You will do the same at the other corners. And when you are back where you started, repeat the same words again. Observe this throughout the ceremony to keep the animals in

front of you at all times, because those who cross might be mad beasts.

Afterwards, circle your horses three times, sprinkling your salt on the animals, saying: "Salt, I throw you from the hand God has given me; Grapin, I take you, of you I await."

In the remainder of your salt, you will bleed the animal used to ride, saying:"Equine beast, I bleed you with the hand that God has given me; Grapin, I take you, of you I await."

It must be bled with a piece of hard wood, such as boxwood or pearwood. Draw as much blood from whatever part you wish, whatever some capricious people may say, who attribute particular virtues to certain parts of the animal. We only recommend that when drawing blood, the animal's ass should be behind you. If it's a sheep, for example, you hold its head between your legs. Finally, after you've bled the animal, collect some of the horn from the right foot with a knife, divide it into two pieces and make a cross out of them; put this cross in a piece of new cloth, then cover it with your salt. Then take some wool, if you are working with sheep; otherwise take horsehair, and make a cross which you place in your cloth on the salt; you then place a second layer of salt on this wool or horsehair. You then make another cross of Paschal virgin wax or blessed candle; then you put the rest of your salt on top of it, and tie the whole thing into a ball with a string. With this ball, you will rub the animals as they leave the stable, if they are horses; if they are sheep, you rub them as they leave the sheepfold or the pen, pronouncing the words you used for the sprinkling of salt. Continue to rub them for 1, 2, 3, 7, 9 or 11 consecutive days. This depends on the strength and vitality of the animals.

Note that you should only do your sprinklings at the last word. When operating on horses, pronounce briskly; when it comes to sheep, the longer you take to pronounce, the better you will do. When you find horsehair in the collection of salt to be cast, you should only do them on salt and not elsewhere. All the guards begin on a Tuesday or a Friday at the crescent of the Moon; and in urgent cases, these observations are overridden. You must be careful not to let your bundles get damp, otherwise the animals would perish. They are usually carried in the gusset, but without burdening yourself with this useless care, do what expert practitioners do. Place them at home in some dry place, and worry not. We said above to take only the horn from the right foot to make the bundle. Most people take horn from all four feet, and consequently make two crosses, since they have four pieces. This is superfluous and produces nothing more. If you do all the ceremonies of the four corners only at the corner of the rising sun, the herd will be less dispersed.

Observe that a wicked shepherd, who has a grudge against the one who replaces him, can cause him much grief, and even cause the flock to perish. Firstly, by means of the bundle, which he cuts into pieces

and scatters, either on a table or elsewhere, or by a rosary novena, after which
he wraps the bundle in it, then cuts the
whole and scatters it, either by means of
a mole or weasel, or by the pot or tare or
cruet, finally by means of a frog or green
treefrog, or a cod tail, which they put into
an anthill, saying: "*Maudition, perdition,
&c.*" They leave it there for nine days,
after which they lift it out again with the
same words, grinding it into powder and
sowing it where the herd is to graze. They
also use three pebbles taken from different cemeteries, and by means of certain
words that we do not wish to reveal, they
provoke emanations, cause scabies, and
make as many animals die as they wish.
We shall hereafter give the way to destroy
these prestiges, by our ways of breaking
guards and all curses.

On this same subject, we intend to re-
print the *Enchridion of Pope Leo*, to which
will be added the discoveries and experiments that Guidon carries out with sur-
prising success.

Guard at one's will.

Astarin, Astaroth who is Bahol, I commit my flock to your charge and custody; and for your wages, I will give you a white or black beast, such as I please. I swear to you, Satarin, that you may guard them for me everywhere in these gardens, while saying hurlupupin.

You will act according to what we have said at the Castle of Belle, and cast the salt, pronouncing the following:

"Gupin shoeing missed the big one; it is Cain who does this to you. You will rub them with the same words."

Another guard.

Woolly beasts, I take you in the name of God and of the most holy sacred Virgin Mary. I pray to God that the bleeding I'm about to do may take and benefit my will. I conjure you that you break and shatter all spells and enchantments which may be passed over the body of my lively flock of woolly beasts, which stand before God and before me, which are in my charge and custody. In the name of the Father, the Son and the Holy Spirit, and of Mr. St John the Baptist and Mr. St Abraham.

See what we have said above about operating at the Castle of Belle, and use the following words for casting and rubbing. *Pass Flori*, Jesus is risen.

Guard against scabies, ringworm and sheep pox.

It was on a Monday morning that the Saviour of the world passed by, the Holy Virgin after him, Mr. St John his shepherd boy, his friend, who seeks his divine flock, which is marred of this evil pox, of which he can no longer endure, because of the three shepherds who went to adore my Saviour Redeemer Jesus Christ in Bethlehem, and who adored the voice of the child. Say *Pater* five times and *Ave* five times.

"My flock will be healthy and pretty, which is subject to me. I pray Madame St Genevieve that she may serve me as a friend here in this malignant pox. Pox banished from God, denied of Jesus Christ, I command you on behalf of the great living God, that you have to depart from here, and that you melt and be confounded before God and before me, as dew melts before the Sun. Most glorious Virgin Mary and the Holy Spirit, pox depart from here, for God command you, as true as Joseph, Nicodemus of Arimathea laid down the precious body of my Saviour and Redeemer Jesus Christ, on Good Friday; from the Tree of the Cross, by the Father, by the Son, by the Holy Spirit, worthy flock of woolly beasts, come hither, approach God and myself. Behold the divine offering of salt that I present to you on this day; as without salt nothing was made, as I believe it, by the Father, &c."

"O salt! I conjure you on behalf of the great living God, that you may serve me for what I claim, that you may preserve and guard my flock from pox, ringworm, scabies, growths, fragility bad waters. I command you, as Jesus Christ my Saviour commanded in the boat to his Disciples, when they said to him: Lord, awake, for the sea frightens us. Immediately the Lord awoke, commanded the sea to stand still: immediately the sea became calm, commanded by the Father, &c."

Before anything else, on this guard, pronounce on the salt:

"*Panem cœlestem accipiat, sit nomen Domine invocabis.*"

Then refer to the Castle of Belle, and do the casting and rubbing while pronouncing the following:

"*Eum ter ergo docentes omnes gentes baptizantes eos. In nomine Patris, &c.*"

Guard against scabies.

When Our Lord ascended to the heavens, his holy virtue on earth left Pasle, Colet and Herve; all that God said has been well said. Red, white or black beasts, of whatever colour you may be, if there is any scabies or mange on you, it was made and put nine feet in the ground, as it is true that it will go away and die, as St John and in his skin and was born in his camel; as Joseph, Nicodemus of Arimathea laid down the body of my sweet Saviour Redeemer Jesus Christ from the tree of the Cross, on Good Friday.

You will use the following words for the casting and the rubbing, and refer to what we have said at the Castle of Belle.

"Salt, I cast you from the hand that God has given me. *Volo et vono Baptista Sancta Agala tum est.*"

Guard to prevent Wolves from entering the land where the Sheep are.

Stand at the quarter of the rising sun, and there pronounce five times the following. If you wish to say it only once, you will do the same five days in a row.

"Come woolly beasts, it is the Lamb of humility, I guard you, *Ave Maria*. This is the Lamb of the Redeemer, who fasted forty days without rebellion, without having taken any rest from the enemy, was tempted in truth. Go straight, you grey, clawed beasts, go get your prey, wolves and she-wolves and cubs, you don't have to come to this meat that is here. In the name of the Father, and of the Son, and of the Holy Spirit, and of the blessed Saint Cerf. So, *vade retro, ô Satana*."

This pronounced at the quarter we have said, continue doing the same at the other quarters; and back where you started, repeat it again. For the remaining, see the Castle of Belle, then make the casting with the follow words:

"*Vanus vanes Christus vaincus,* attack salt *soli*, attack Saint Sylvain in the name of Jesus."

The Puppets guards.

We go, we go to them, let us marry and let us marry them, we unbind ourselves and we marry them to Beelzebuth.

This guard is dangerous and embarrassing, or rather its success is very uncertain; it requires a very pure disposition of the soul, for it to succeed.

Guard for Horses.

Salt, who is made and formed from the foam of the sea, I conjure you to make my happiness and the profit of my master; I conjure you in the name of Crouay; Don, I conjure you in the name of Crouay; Satan, I conjure you in the name of Crouay; Leot, I conjure you in the name of Crouay; Valiot, I conjure you in the name of Crouay; Rou and Rouvayet, come hither, I take you for my valets. Cast. *Festi Christi* Belial.

Restrain from saying: *Rouvayet, what you will do, I will find it well made;* because this guard is also strong, and sometimes even tiresome. Refer to what was said at the Castle of Belle, concerning guards.

Guard for the flock.

All beasts of prey that might attack this lively flock of woolly beasts, let them be bridled by the *hoc est enim Corpus meum.* Woolly beasts, come to me, here is an offering of salt that I present to you, and which I will give you, in the name of God and the Virgin, and of Mr. St John. Woolly beasts, come to me, and turn to me. Here is an offering of salt blessed by God, which I will give you, deliver and cast, in the name of God, the Virgin and Mr. St John. Woolly beasts, come to me, here is an offering of salt blessed by God, which I present to you and will deliver and cast upon you. Lively flock of woolly beasts, here present before God and before me, in the name of God and the Virgin, and of Mr. St John; may this salt keep them for me healthy and clean, well-drinking , well-eating , fat and large, low and swallowed, well closed and enclosed around me, as is the lamb of Mr. St John. And to his honour, I believe this salt keep them for me healthy and clean, well-drinking, well-eating, fat and large, low and swallowed, well closed and enclosed around me, as is the lamb of Mr. St John. I believe that this salt will keep them clear and shiny, to please everyone, in the name of God and the Virgin, and of Mr. St John. I believe that this salt will protect them from wolves and she-wolves, and from all the beasts of prey who prowl day and night. Blessed salt of God, I conjure you that you will grant it to me; for I believe in it, in the name of

God, of the Virgin and of Mr. St John. O great God, I believe that this salt will preserve them from scabies, mange, pox, and any evil that may befall the body of this lively flock of woolly beasts. Blessed salt of God, I believe you will do this in the name of God and the Virgin, and of Mr. St John. Amen.

A Mass of the Holy Spirit must be said over the salt; it must begin with the *Confiteor,* and continue to the end. You can say it yourself. For the remainder, you will proceed as in the Castle of Belle, and use the following words for the casting, etc.

"*Vamus Jesus Christus et memores*, attack salt *seli*, attack St Sylvain in the name of Jesus."

Another guard for the Sheep.

Salt, who has been created by God and blessed by his most worthy hand, I conjure you by the great living God, and of Mr. St Riquier, who is the fighter of all

Devils. I conjure you that you may break and corrupt all words that have been said, read and celebrated over the body of this lively flock of woolly beasts, which is here present before God and before me. Salt which is made by God and blessed by his worthy hand, I conjure, present and apply on the body of this lively flock, that is here before God and before me. It is my intention and desire, that you keep them healthy and clean, fat, large and round; that they be well enclosed around me, like the belt of the most sacred Virgin Mary, when she carried the body of my sweet Saviour Redeemer Jesus Christ. *Casta sacravera viga corpus Domini nostri Jesus Christi qui tima menta Deus; in nomine Patri, et Filii, et Spiritus Sancti.* Amen.

For its application, refer to what is taught at the Castle of Belle, and use for the casting and rubbing the following words, or those of the above casts that suits you, *passe Flori,* Jesus is risen.

New guard for Sheep, taught by the learned Bellerot, in his treatise on the preservation of woolly beasts.

Get a church candle which will have been used for the first Easter communion of a young girl born to wise and virtuous parents. Light it and place it into the earth, not far from a river or a stream, where you will lead your sheep to pasture. Trace a large semicircle capable of enclosing your whole flock, and for that, use a mystical rod. This being done, sit on an earth bank, which you will have arranged beforehand and after you have commended yourself to the Most Holy Trinity, you will make the three calls marked in the *Red Dragon*, page 30 and following, taking care to always have in hand the mysterious rod of which we have just spoken in order to carry out its destined use.

The Spirit will appear to you and you will command him to touch each of the sheep present and to commit unto him, or one of his subordinates, now and forever, to the protection of your flock, which he will do immediately.

What we have given about guards should be enough to satisfy both shepherd and groom, since a guard intended for one can serve the other, merely changing the name of the lively flock of woolly animals to that of equine beasts. However, it is worth to note that the stronger and more tiresome a guard is, the more suitable it is for horses, and the softer and sweeter the guard, the more suitable it is for sheep. And so that the labourer may earn some particular fruit from our discoveries, we will continue with a guard which concerns him particularly. It is of an infinite resource for those who are close to rabbit warrens. The animals will not be able to damage the crop, observing what we are going to teach. On the contrary, they will destroy all the weeds in the grain you want to protect.

Guard against Rabbits.

Take salt in a plate or dish: the quantity cannot be determined as it will depend on the extent of the land you wish to preserve. In addition, have some rabbit droppings, and five pieces of tiles collected at a procession or in a cemetery, then being in the place where you want to perform this experiment. You will begin on the side of the rising sun, bareheaded and kneeling. You will say the following and make the crosses on the salt: † dant † dant † dant † sant † Heliot, and Valiot; Rouvayet, come hither, I take you for my valet, to guard here against these accursed rabbits and doe, may they have to cross and pass through this field (name the grain) which is here present before God and before myself, without causing any harm or damage; that they be bridled on behalf of Reveillot; for I command and conjure you on behalf of the great living God, to obey me, you and your companions, to do what I am going to ask of

you ; that is to keep for three months and three moons this field of N., here present before God and me, as I believe by the faith that I have in you. Thus, I believe that you will do it. Thus I believe by the virtue of this blessed salt of God, and of the tiles and droppings of the accursed beasts, rabbits and doe. Thus I believe by all the forces and powers you may have over them. Thus I do believe.

Dig a hole in the earth, put a dropping in it, saying; "Rou and Rouvayet, come hither, I take you for my valet."

Put a pinch of salt on the dropping, saying: "Salt, I place you from the hand that God has given me, Rou and Rouvayet, come hither, I take you for my valet."

Then lay a tile, saying: "Tile, I place you from the hand that God has given me."

Strike the tile with your left heel, making a right turn, saying: "Rou and Rouvayet, come hither, I take you for my valet."

Do the same at the other three corners, then cross the middle of the field, where you do as when at one of the corners, then from this middle, return to the first corner to begin your throws; at the first you will say: "Salt, I cast you from the hand that God has given me, anchor to the Virgin."

Continue your throws around the place, saying only: After the first anchor to the Virgin. Returning to where you started, take the remaining of your salt and make a single throw, saying: "Rou and Rouvayet, come hither, I take you for my valet."

If the land is divided into different parcels and of different grains, you must perform the same ceremonies for each place; instead of three months and three moons, you will name what you please.

We propose to give guards of another kind in the French Translation of Agrippa, and in the Clavicles of Solomon. To these works, we will add secrets of our own experience.

To bridle.

Take two small pieces of straw; one must have a knot in the middle, put the other one over the knot to form a cross, then pronounce on it:

"Anchor of God, anchor of the Virgin, anchor of the devil; Satan, be gone to all the devils."

Then, throw the cross at the animal, pronouncing the same words with one knee on the ground. By this means, you can carry the animal, however vicious it may be, on your shoulders or otherwise, without the risk of being bitten.

To be hard.

Valanda jacem rafit massif excorbis anter valganda zazar, brother lend me your hand; Bourbelet, Barlet, Amer gather around me, as Judas betrayed our Lord.

Wear the note around your neck, and in danger, pronounce the same words. It was by this means that Guidon, attacked by two cavalrymen at an inn in Fauville, saved himself from a good five hundred sabre blows; after this assault, he returned quietly to his house.

To discover Treasures.

Being at the place where a treasure is suspected to be, say, stumping three times with the left heel against the ground, and making a turn to the left:

"Sadies satani agir fons toribus: come to me, Seradon, who shall be called Sarietur."

Repeat three times in succession. If there is any treasure at that place, you will know it, because something will be revealed to your ear.

To stop Horses, crew and lead a
person astray.

Trace on black paper in white ink the
pentacle figured on the cover of this
book. Throw the pentacle thus traced at

the head of the horses, and say: "White or
black horse, of whatever colour you may
be, it is I who make you do it, I conjure
you so you may not pull anymore with

your feet as you do with your ears, nor can Beelzebuth break his chain." For this experiment, you will need a nail forged during midnight mass, which you will drive where the harness passes through. Failing that, take a scab and conjure it as follows:

"Scab, I conjure you in the name of Lucifer, Beelzebuth and Satanas, the three Princes of all devils, that you must stop."

During the three days before the day you wish to perform this operation, be careful not to do any Christian work.

Counter-Charm.

Hostia sacra verra corrum, while repelling the great devil of hell, all words, enchantments and characters that have been said, read and celebrated on the bodies of my lively horses, may they be broken and shattered behind me.

After this, repeat the orison which begins with these words: "*Word, which has become flesh, &c.*"

So that the Lambs come back
beautiful and strong.

Take the first-born; failing that, the first to come to you. Lift it from the ground with its nose towards you, then say:

"Ecce lignum crucem in quo salus mundi crucem."

Put it back on the ground, lift it up again and say as above; do the same three times. When you have done this, you will pronounce with a low voice the orison of the day for the current day.

Against firearm.

Star which leads the weapon today, may I charm thee, I say to thee, may thou obey me; in the name of the Father, and of the Son, and Sanatatis. Make the sign of the Cross.

Against ulcerous lesions; fevers.

Take the first sheep afflicted by the said disease. Facing the rising sun, open its mouth and say inside the following words three times:

"Brac, Cabrac, Carabra, Cadebrac, Cabracam, I heal you."

Blow into the sheep's mouth each time, and release it among the others. They will all be healed. You need to make as many signs of the Cross as there are afflicted sheep. These same words, written on paper and worn around the neck for nine days, cure fever.

Against glanders and colic in Horses.

Horse (name the hair) belonging to N., if you have glanders, of whatever colour they may be, and abdominal cramps or colic, or of thirty-six kinds of other ailments, for whatever they may be, may God heal you as well as blessed Saint Eloy: in the name of the Father, and of the Son, and of the Holy Spirit. Then say five times *Pater* and *Ave, &c.*, on your knees.

As soon as you have pronounced these words, if the horse has glanders, you have to inject the following decoction into its throat with a syringe:

Take elderflower, chamomile, a handful of each; simmer them lightly in two pints of water, filter the whole and add half an ounce of ammonia salt, three ounces of anti-scorbutic syrup and half a pint of vinegar. Repeat the words and injections several times a day.

If it is afflicted with colic, instead of the above remedy, employ the following:

After bleeding the horse, make him swallow a pound of olive oil, and give it some linseed enemas.

To heal strains and sprains in Horses.

Atay de satay suratay avalde, walk. Repeat three times, striking the hoof of the horse. If it is on the side of the saddle, strike with the left foot.

At the same time, apply a compress of vinegar around the fetlock in which you have boiled sage and rosemary. This compress must be renewed each time it cools down. You will also do well to make the animal bleed from the neck.

To prevent a flock from touching the grain, passing between two furrows.

Take a silver coin, hang it around the neck of one of the sheep, saying the following nine times:

"Satan, Satourne, speaking of Grica-cœur da voluptere Lord of Nazariau; I request and command you, and humbly conjure, that you have to come and guard and make my lively flock of woolly beasts pass in the evening, day and morning, saying hurlupupin."

We don't want to say anything more about these words of ingratiation.

To pass the hemorrhaging..

Take the afflicted beast and say the following words three times over its head: "*In tes dalame bouis, vins Divernas Sathan.*"

Against pulmonary disease.

Open the mouth of the horse, blow into it three times and say the above words.

Against mumps.

Take some holy water with the tip of your finger, and touching the undersides of the jaws, say:

† *Christus Brutus et datus et vanum.*

Against scabies and ringworm in animals.

Gupin shœing missed the big one; it is Cain who does this to you. Take some sulphur flowers with oil and a pinch of salt, make an ointment from it, with which you will rub the animals, while pronouncing the words above. Repeat until healed.

Against hemorrhoids.

With the middle finger of the left hand, some saliva to your mouth, and touch the hemorrhoids with it, saying:

"Pins, begone, God curses you; in the name of the Father, the Son, and the Holy Spirit." Then say *Pater* and *Ave* nine times for nine days. The second day, say only eight, and decrease the number of times each day, in order.

Twice in a day, you should rub the hemorrhoids with some fresh butter in which you will have cooked some inner bark from the elder tree.

Against epilepsy or falling sickness.

Place the epileptic in a well-ventilated place, rub his forearms and say in his right ear: "*Oremus præceptis salutaris moniti.*"

Add the Dominical Prayer. Before these prayers have been completed, the sick person will rise.

A sovereign remedy against the falling sickness is water which flows from an incision made in a lime tree in February; it is given each time in the quantity of three ounces.

Enchantment to stop blood.

Sanguis manè in te sicut fecit Christus in sanguis manè in tua vena sicut Christus in sua

pœnat sanguis manè fixus sicut quando fuit cruci-
fixus.

Repeat three times.

Counter-Charm..

*E*cce Crucem Domini, fugite partes adversae,
vicit leo de Tribu Juda, radix David.

Against fire.

*I*n te, Domine, speravi, non confundar in
aeternum.

Against fevers.

God came into the world to redeem us from our sins: he fasted thirty-three years and three days: he was sold to the Jews for thirty deniers, tertian Fever, quartan Fever, Fever of whatever quality it may be, cannot remain on my body:

in the name of Jesus, who was tied to the tree of the Cross, where he shed his blood only for our sins. Holy Mary, pray for me: Saint Michael, preserve me, Jesus, Maria, Saint Joseph, help me; Mary Saint Catherine, preserve me.

Here must be placed the name of the Contributor, who must wear the above around his neck, saying every day while fasting five *Pater* and five *Ave* in front of an image of the Virgin.

TABLE.

COLLECTION OF THE RAREST SECRETS
OF THE MAGICAL ART